Prayers of the Way

Prayers of the Way

Daily prayers and meditations
for groups and individuals

John Johansen-Berg

EPWORTH PRESS

ISBN 0 7162 0482 7

First published 1992
by Epworth Press
1 Central Buildings, Westminster,
London S W1H 9 N R

Typeset at The Spartan Press, Lymington, Hants
and printed in Great Britain by
Mackays of Chatham, Kent

Contents

These readings from the Gospels of Luke, John and Matthew recount the expectation and birth of Jesus of Nazareth, the child born to be the Saviour of the world. Matthew, with his story of the wise men from the east, the homely account of Luke and the sublime theology of John combine to bring us to the heart of the meaning of Advent and Christmas.

The readings are taken from St John's Gospel, followed by a comment and prayer on the theme. This is a deeply spiritual gospel which gives us a precious glimpse into the inner life of Jesus and expresses many of his great claims. In a generation of spiritual searching, meditations on St John's account of Jesus will be particularly helpful. Some of the other prayers are based on Psalms, Ephesians and Revelation.

The readings are from St Luke's Gospel, followed by a comment and prayer on the theme. Luke's account is a very personal one, appreciative of the significance of women and children and conscious of the value of individual people. It has a strong liberation emphasis and gives a historical setting to the story. The teaching of Jesus comes over with as sharp a challenge and relevance as it must have had in his own day.

Dedicated
to my mother,
whose love and support
have been a constant encouragement

Preface

This prayer book has been written for individuals and groups to share in daily prayers based on passages in the Gospels, including material for the Christmas season.

Each day has an opening meditation verse, an introduction from a psalm or other biblical verses, a Bible reading and meditation words, prayers and closing benediction. It is envisaged that there will be periods of silence, especially after the readings, and that there may be music, songs and free prayers, particularly relevant intercessions. Though particularly useful for ecumenical groups, the prayers are also suitable for individual meditation and worship. The benedictions are printed in 'you' form but can be used with 'we' and 'us' when appropriate.

Some of the readings are short so it is recommended that use is made of an additional reading from a suitable lectionary. When used by groups, the reading may be followed by a response such as L. 'This is the word of the Lord.' R. 'Thanks be to God.' or L. 'This is the gospel of Christ.' R. 'Praise to Christ our Lord.' Meditations on the readings and a responsive version of the psalm verses are available from the Community for Reconciliation.

Usually the first prayer follows the theme of the reading. Other prayers may be meditations, intercessions, or on such themes as mission and peace, and the Lord's Prayer. As intercessions mainly arise from particular circumstances, it is suggested that the service should often include a time of free prayer or particular intercessions expressed by the worship leader.

The Prayers for the Day are additional prayers given in the appendix. These are ancient prayers of the church plus a prayer which is used when lighting a candle for peace. The Universal Prayer for Peace, recommended for use each day following the response, is the final prayer in the appendix. Spoken in many languages, it unites people of different nations and faiths who long for and pray for peace in our world.

Material from Genesis, Exodus and Isaiah together with the Acts of the Apostles, Ephesians and Holy Week material complete a six month cycle with an appendix giving dates throughout the year. Information about this is available from the Community.

Some of the material was originally written for use in the daily worship of the Community for Reconciliation, an ecumenical Christian community committed to mission, peace and reconciliation.

'Live in peace and the God of love and peace will be with you.'

John Johansen-Berg
August 1992

Barnes Close
Chadwich, Nr Bromsgrove,
Worcs B61 0RA

Acknowledgments

I express my thanks to various friends who have helped with the production of drafts, especially to Maggie Hamilton whose patient work on the computer, spending many hours to produce the revisions and re-drafts, has enabled the completion of the final draft for the publisher.

The meditation words for each day are taken from the Holy Bible, New International Version, © 1973, 1978, 1984 by the International Bible Society. They are used by permission of Hodder and Stoughton Ltd.

The Nativity Accounts

Day 1: December 22   The Annunciation

White foaming riders on the sea, sign of God's glory
   White cloudy racers high in the sky, sign of God's splendour
Angelic messengers on earth, bearers of God's news
   Waiting people in many places, hearers of God's word.

Isaiah 9.2–3   Prayer for the Day   Reading: Luke 1.26–38

Meditation words: *You will be with child and give birth to a son, and you are to give him the name Jesus.*

Holy God,
      We give you thanks for Mary
         who was so ready to be obedient to you;
      we thank you for her purity and humility,
         for her faith and her joy.
      As she was ready to put her trust in you
         so may we be faithful
               and ready to work in the way you direct,
         knowing that nothing is impossible with you.

We hold before you, Lord,
      all those for whom the winter brings difficulties;
      the elderly for whom icy pavements are a danger,
      the disabled trapped at home by snow;
      the blind who face extra hazards in winter
      and the lonely whose solitude seems worse in cold
                                    conditions.
May the darkness of winter be enlightened by your presence
      and the promise of spring never be forgotten.

I search, Lord, through the book of my memories
and am greatly encouraged by times past;
by friends whose support encourages me;
by acquaintances whose story is an inspiration;
by speakers and preachers with a worthwhile message
to proclaim.

But most of all I recall with gratitude
all the times when your presence has sustained me
in springtime and winter, in sorrow and joy.

Response

L: When your messenger brings your word to us

R: Make us ready to respond with faith and joy.

Prayer for Peace

*May the divine Potter fashion you for his eternal plan;
break you and remake you in his divine image;
melt you and mould you for his own praise.
May Father, Son and Spirit create you anew each day.*

Loving God, giving the spark of life to all creation
Living God, giving the fire of love to all people
Spirit of God, bestowing the spark of life in birth
Spirit of God, sustaining the search for justice and for truth.

Isaiah 9.6–7a   Prayer for the Day   Reading: Luke 1.39–55

Meditation words: *He has brought down rulers from their thrones but has lifted up the humble.*

Great and mighty God,
    You are the Holy One in our midst;
        your mercy is experienced in every generation;
    you bring down the proud and raise up the humble.
    You tumble monarchs from their thrones
        but raise up those of no account.
    You send away the rich empty-handed
        but you pour out blessings for the poor.
    You have a plan to help your chosen nation
        and to bless abundantly all nations.
    We are filled with joy because you are our Saviour;
        you have done and shall do great things
        for us and all your people.

Loving Lord,
    we hold before you the hungry;
        you show how much you care for them;
        so may we too show concern by loving action.
    We hold before you the poor;
        you show your care for them;
        so may we too show our care by sharing.

We hold before you the people of our community
    who have a special task, job or position.
As all people are special to you
    we pray that you will bless each according to their need.

Creator God,
    in the midst of the turmoil of our times
      we seek your guidance and help.
At night we meditate, looking up at the night sky;
      the myriad stars of light remind us of your love
          in sending your Son to overcome the darkness.
In the quietness we commit our lives to you
      and we feel assurance that through the times of turmoil
        you will be with us,
        you will guide and enable us
        and all will be well.

Response

L: When we meet with others on spiritual pilgrimage

R: **May we recognize and encourage each other in the journey of
    faith.**

Prayer for Peace

*May the God who inspired Mary's magnificat bless you
May the Son whose birth filled Mary with joy bless you
May the Spirit who overshadowed Mary bless you
May the Most High bless your coming and your going.*

Day 3:   December 24   The Dream

In our visions are the hopes for a new world
    In our dreams are the glimpses of a new era
Speak, Lord, in the dreams and visions of your people
    May we realize our hopes by fulfilling your purpose.

Isaiah 9.7b   **Prayer for the Day**   **Reading:** Matthew 1.18–25

Meditation words: *Joseph son of David, do not be afraid to take Mary home as your wife, because what is conceived in her is from the Holy Spirit.*

Holy God,
    you speak to us so often in dreams or visions
        and sometimes the message seems beyond belief
            or the news so good that we doubt its authenticity.
    Help us to put aside our doubts and hesitations;
    inspire us to hear your word, to believe it
        and to live out our discipleship,
            putting our trust in you.

I watch a robin, Father,
    and it seems such an insignificant creature
        as it hops about searching for something to eat.
Yet this little bird expresses the heart of your creation
    for in its throbbing life your love is expressed.
When we respond to its need
    by throwing some bread to fall on the snow beside it,
        we express your compassion to all living creatures.
So, watching the robin,
    I meditate on the wonder of your world.

We look forward, God of the Universe, with eager
expectation
to all that you will do for your people.
As long ago men and women waited
and found fulfilment of your promise
in the coming of Jesus into the world,
so may we look forward, confidently,
knowing that Jesus will return again.
Come quickly, Lord, come.

Response

L: In a world where mistrust and failure fill us with despair

R: Help us to see the miracles which bring unfailing hope.

Prayer for Peace

May the Father give you hope in searching
May the Son give you faith in questing
May the Spirit give you joy in finding
May the Holy Trinity go with you on your journey.

Day 4:   December 25   The Birth

God of the changing scene,
You walk with us on the pilgrimage of life
You stay with us from birth to death
You are the joy of the journey's beginning
And you are the peace at the journey's end.

Isaiah 11.1–3a   Prayer for the Day   Reading: Luke 2.1–7

Meditation words: *She wrapped him in cloths and placed him in a manger, because there was no room for them in the inn.*

Holy God,
    we recall the wonder of that moment
        in a little village in Palestine many years ago
            when you gave to the world your Son.
    It was a time of sheer joy
        for all who realized something of what was happening
    and a moment of great significance
        for all the world.
    Help us to know the same happiness
        whenever we celebrate the birthday of your Son.

Holy Spirit,
    we pray for the United Nations Organization,
        its Secretary-General and all the representatives.
    Guide them in all their deliberations
        that they may seek to establish justice and peace.
    May all those involved in the specialized agencies
        express common care and mutual concern.
    May we work together in the family of nations
        to overcome the ancient enemies –
            hunger, poverty and disease –
        and to establish a world of health and true welfare.

Jesus, Prince of Peace
> as you were welcomed long ago
>   by those who saw in your coming
>   light for the nations,
> so we welcome your influence
>   in our world and in our nation,
>   in our family and in our lives.
> By your inspiration may there be
>   peace amongst all people.

Response

L: When the star shone brightly in Bethlehem

R: New hope dawned for a waiting world.

Prayer for Peace

May the God of Sarah and Abraham walk with you on pilgrimage
May the God of Rebecca and Isaac bless you and your family
May the God of Mary and Joseph reveal to you his salvation
*   and may your years be blessed with the divine presence.*

Day 5: December 26   The Word

Before time began, Thou art
  Before anything was created, Thou art
In the silence, Thou hast spoken
  From the chaos, Thou hast made order.

Isaiah 11.3b–5   **Prayer for the Day**   **Reading: John 1.1–13**

Meditation words: *In the beginning was the Word, and the Word was with God, and the Word was God.*

Creator God,
    you are from all time
        the ground of the universe,
        the beginning and the end.
    You gave your Word to the world
        and in that Word we find light and life.

Loving Jesus,
    you shared with your Father
        in making a world to be at peace;
    you call people to live in harmony.
    Forgive us for turning from your peace
        to our division, hostility and enmity.
    Grant us to be at one with you
        and with all people
    that in your presence we may have
        the peace that passes understanding.

Holy Spirit,
    around us is a world of need,
        with many people facing sadness and despair.
    Whilst some people have much to eat and drink
        others lack the necessities for life.

In cities thronged with people
    there are many who are lonely and in trouble.
Amidst the selfishness and greed
    there is a deep longing for true meaning.
Help us to proclaim the good news
        so that women, men and children may find in Christ
            the way to life and an experience of joy.

Response

L: Holy God, you spoke to us in time through your living Word;

R: Help us to respond in time, that by your Word we may come to eternal life.

Prayer for Peace

May the God of eternity bless you through the years
May the God of time bless you all your days
May the God who is Alpha be with you all your life
May the God who is Omega be with you to your end.

Day 6: December 27   Made Flesh

From mineral, soil and water, earth was made
     From flesh and bone, humankind was made
Into the earth came the divine Word
     Into human flesh came the divine child.

Isaiah 11.6–7   **Prayer for the Day**   **Reading:** John 1.14–18

Meditation words: *The Word became flesh and made his dwelling among us . . . full of grace and truth.*

Father,
     your Son took flesh and became one of us
         that he might bring light in darkness
             and hope to overcome despair.
He came into the world
     and the world rejected him.
But your love keeps reaching out
     to draw us to yourself.
By your grace we dimly perceive your glory,
     the glory of the Father in the Son.

Dearest Jesus,
     you long for your people to live in peace;
yet in many parts of the world
     division and enmity mar our society.
Forgive us, Lord, our hard-heartedness
     and turn us to yourself;
in you may we find peace –
     your peace to be shared with those around us.

Holy God,
>   you sent your prophets with a message
>>   and the world would not listen;
>   you sent your Son into the world
>>   and the world did not recognize him;
>   you sent Jesus to express your love
>>   and your people crucified him.
>   We have rejected you; but you never reject us.
>>   You go on loving until we respond.
>   Help us to return your love
>>   and to proclaim it to a waiting world.

Response

L: Living Lord, you entered into our world of flesh and blood, of birth and death;

R: **Prepare a place for us in your world of spirit and truth, of joy and peace.**

Prayer for Peace

> *Walk in the light and the light will illumine your path*
> *Walk in the truth and the truth will set you free*
> *Walk the way of peace and you will have through Christ*
>   *the peace that passes understanding.*

Day 7: December 28   The Shepherds

Be with us in the lighting of the fire, eternal light
Be with us in the work throughout the day
Be with us in the keeping of the flocks, divine Shepherd
Be with us in the watches of the night.

Isaiah 11.8–9   **Prayer for the Day**   **Reading:** Luke 2.8–20

Meditation words: *And there were shepherds living out in the fields near by, keeping watch over their flocks at night.*

Loving God,
> we give you thanks for the shepherds in the fields
>> who so gladly heard and responded
>>> to the news of the birth of the Saviour.
> Keep us honest and industrious in doing our work;
> keep us alert, ready to hear your messengers;
> make us eager and active in responding to your word;
> give us faithfulness in sharing the good news with others;
> fill us with joy in our meeting with the Christ-child.
> May our praise and worship be offered for your glory.

Shepherd Jesus
> we hold before you all those who care for animals,
>> especially in these winter months.
> We remember the farmers
>> who endure discomfort and take risks
>>> to make sure that the cattle are sheltered and fed.

We remember the shepherds
>who go out in winter storms
>to bring the sheep to a place of safety.
Be with them in their daily work,
>guarding and guiding them, inspiring and enabling
>>them.

Holy Spirit,
>we rejoice that you came upon Mary,
>>overshadowing her with your power and love
so that in the fullness of time
>Jesus was born,
>>hope of the world, light of the nations,
>>our Saviour and our Lord.

Response

L: Lord, when in the night watches we wait upon you

R: **Reveal to our inner being the mystery of your love.**

Prayer for Peace

May the light of the sky give you hope
May the sound of the seas give you inspiration
May the scent of the earth surround you with joy
May the God of all creation bless you through all your days.

Day 8: December 29   Simeon and Anna

In the quiet of the morning, know that God is here
In the quiet of the evening, know that God is with you
Through the silence of the years of waiting
Be still and know that all will be fulfilled.

Luke 1.68–69   Prayer for the Day   Reading: Luke 2.22–38

Meditation words: *She never left the temple but worshipped night and day, fasting and praying.*

Creator God,
    we give you thanks that in every generation
        there are those who wait upon you,
            attentive to your call and living to your glory.
    We thank you for Simeon and Anna
        whose life of prayer and worship
            kept them close to you, ready to respond.
    We thank you that they were there at the temple
            to greet the infant Jesus
            and welcome him to a world of need.
    Keep us like them, faithful in prayer, prepared for service
        and ready to be moved by the Spirit to welcome Jesus
            in whose name we offer you our prayers.

Dear Lord,
    there are many who are vulnerable in our society,
        not least children in need.
    We pray for those who are orphans,
        deprived of parents by war or disaster;
    for those in hospitals and orphanages,
        especially any suffering from neglect
            or lacking needed medical help.

We pray for all those who care for children
in institutions and in the community.
Give them skill and love in their service.
Children are so precious a gift, Lord;
help us to share gladly in common concern for their
welfare
and assure all your children of your presence and love.

Holy Spirit,
long ago you revealed to Simeon
that he would greet the promised Christ
and you prompted him to go to the temple
to welcome the Saviour in that holy place.
Descend upon us
to make us more aware of your divine purpose,
to enable us for service in the world,
to inspire us in our prayer and worship
and to instil in us your compassion and goodness.

Response

L: Prince of peace, your people wait for you in many places;

R: Speak your word of assurance that we shall welcome you
as you welcome us to your kingdom.

Prayer for Peace

May you find peace in the journey and the destination
May you find peace in the aim and the achievement
May you find peace in the beginning and the end
May God, Father, Son and Spirit give you peace
now and always.

Day 9:   December 30   The Wise Men

Bright star of the heavens, lead us in your way
Lone star of the night sky, guide us by your light
Illumine the quest for truth
and guide us to our destination.

Luke 1.76–79   **Prayer for the Day**   **Reading:** Matthew 2.1–12

Meditation words: *When they saw the star, they were overjoyed.*

God of wisdom,
　　we thank you for the wise men and women of every
　　　　　　　　　　　　　　　　　　　　　generation,
　　　　especially for those who seek spiritual wisdom.
　　We thank you for those wise men
　　　　whose study of your word and your world
　　　　　　prepared them for the coming of Jesus.
　　We thank you that they were watching for the star,
　　　　your sign in the night sky,
　　　　　　and that they followed it to Bethlehem.
　　Teach us your truth and wisdom;
　　　　make us ready to see your signs in the sky and on earth;
　　may we share in the joy of the wise men
　　　　as we too make our offering
　　　　　　in glad response to your gift of love.

In the cold of winter
　　we hold before you, loving Lord, all those who are
　　　　　　　　　　　　　　　　　　　　　homeless,
　　　　sleeping in shop doorways, in cold cellars,
　　　　in old attics, in draughty stations.

We pray for the elderly homeless
   who have little prospect of rebuilding their lives;
we pray for the homeless young,
   disillusioned and despairing in a callous world.
Inspire your people, Lord,
   to offer shelter to the homeless,
   a place of welcome to the friendless
   and a place of hope to those in bleak despair.

Holy Spirit,
   you guide your people into truth,
      you warn your people of danger.
As you guided wise men to Bethlehem,
      as you warned them in a dream not to go back to Herod,
so guard us from the dangers of this generation,
so guide us in our quest for truth
and help us to show in our lives
      faithfulness and gentleness.

Response

L: When we search for you in the darkness and despair

R: Show us the star of hope which brings us light.

Prayer for Peace

May the light of God illumine your path
May Christ, the light of the world, make your life radiant
May the star of the Spirit make the night bright as the day for you
May Father, Son and Spirit illumine your pilgrim way.

Day 10: December 31 The Flight into Egypt

Lord, you are with us in the flight across field and fen
You go before us across moor and cliff
When oppressors and tyrants pursue the innocent
You sustain, you guide, you uphold your people.

Luke 1.46b–50 **Prayer for the Day Reading:** Matthew 2.13–18

Meditation words: *He was furious, and he gave orders to kill all the boys in Bethlehem and its vicinity who were two years old and under.*

Loving Father,
>how you must grieve
>>when your people are so cruel to each other.
>You sent your Son to redeem the world
>>and one of our first responses
>>>was the massacre of innocent children.
>How you must grieve
>>that in every generation there has been cruelty,
>>>the torture and killing of defenceless people.
>Lord, forgive us.

Friend of the lonely,
>we remember that in infancy
>>you were taken by Mary and Joseph
>>>to the land to Egypt, journeying as a refugee family.
>We pray for all who are refugees today,
>>the victims of enmity and war,
>>the sufferers from ethnic violence and hostility,
>>>oppressed by cruel regimes and callous leaders,
>>>fleeing before advancing armies.
>Be near to comfort and strengthen them.

May the nations of the world
    be ready to give sanctuary to refugees.
May there soon be throughout our world
    a new time of freedom, justice and harmony
        so that no one is driven from home and country.

God of the pilgrim way,
    we thank you that your love found fulfilment
        in sending into a world of need
           the child born to be redeemer and saviour.
    Give us such a sense of your presence
        that we may have an inner peace,
      such a reponse to your love
        that we may serve those in deepest need,
      such an experience of your joy
        that we may bring smiles to the faces of the
                              oppressed.

Response

L: When tyrants rage and oppressors threaten

R: **Give to your people a quiet assurance of your presence and
your power.**

Prayer for Peace

*As the tree gives you shade in the heat of noonday
As the cave gives you shelter in the midst of the storm
As the rock gives you safety in the rising waters
As the church gives you sanctuary when oppressors pursue
So may God keep you safe in his loving care.*

Day 11: January 1   The Child Jesus

> *You are the hope of the rainbow's arch*
> *You are the light in the candle's flame*
> *You are the laughter in the child's eyes*
> *Yours is the love that calls my name.*

Luke 1.51–55   **Prayer for the Day**   **Reading:** Luke 2.41–52

Meditation words: *Everyone who heard him was amazed at his understanding and his answers.*

Divine Father of every family,
    we give you thanks for Mary and Joseph;
        for their love so freely given to Jesus;
        for their obedience to you and readiness to serve you;
        for their joy in all the responsibilities of parenthood.
We thank you for the childhood of Jesus;
        for his understanding, his obedience, his humility
        and his patience in waiting for the time of his ministry.
May we look to Jesus
    and find in him our example and inspiration;
may we too be ready to be used
    where you will and how you will
    for the glory of your name.

Life-giving Spirit,
    in every generation you call and equip
        those who are to be ministers of the gospel
            and pastors for the people.
Guide and enable all those called into various ministries
                            today.
As they serve in local churches, in hospitals and colleges,
    may they teach the faith wisely,
    may they preach the gospel faithfully,
    may they celebrate the sacraments joyfully,

may they serve the needy compassionately,
may they confront injustice prophetically,
may they care for their people pastorally.
In all their word and work of ministry
may they have your gifts and show your fruit
to the glory of God our Creator
and in the name of Jesus our Saviour.

Holy Spirit,
at the beginning of a new year
fall afresh on your people.
Make us joyful in our witness to Jesus Christ;
make us compassionate in our service to those in need;
give us power in the proclamation of good news
and courage as servants of the kingdom.
Endow us with the spiritual gifts we need
for our pilgrimage of faith
and help us to show your fruit of love, joy and peace.

Response

L: Lord, in the love of our home and the fellowship of the church

R: Help us to know your presence, your power and your peace.

Prayer for Peace

In your rising each new dawn, may Christ be with you
In your work through every day, may Christ be with you
In the rest you take at night, may Christ be with you
The blessing of the Father, Son and Spirit
be yours now and always.

The Life and Ministry of Jesus

Day 12

In the desert hear the wind over the sands
In the wilderness experience the quiet over the land
In the wasteland hear the voice of God
In the wilderness experience God's presence and his peace.

Psalm 29.5–9   **Prayer for the Day**   **Reading:** John 1.19–28

Meditation words: *John replied . . . 'I am the voice of one calling in the desert.'*

Father,
    you sent your servant John
        to proclaim Jesus, the Lamb of God.
    John came as the voice in the wilderness,
        proclaiming the way of the Lord.
    We thank you for the messengers of old;
        we thank you for the sending of your Son.
    We pray that you will keep us faithful
        as your messengers today.

God of Righteousness,
    hear me when I call to you.
    Help me to dismiss selfish anger from my thinking;
    lead me to commune with you in silence;
    fill my heart with joy
        as I recall your many blessings.
    In peace I will arise in the morning;
        in peace I will lie down to sleep.
    For you alone, O God, are my safety and my rest.

Teacher Jesus,
    you sent out your disciples two by two
        to proclaim your kingdom and to heal the sick.
    We cannot fail to go out in faith
        when you commission and enable us.

Send us in your power
to proclaim your word,
knowing that according to your promise
you walk with us on the pilgrim's way.

Response

L: When the people call out in anguish

R: **Our God will hear and answer.**

Prayer for Peace

The blessing of the One be with you in your solitude
The blessing of the Three be with you in community
The blessing of the Creator refresh you in your discipleship
The blessing of Father, Son and Spirit
keep you in the communion of saints.

Day 13

Creator God, open our ears to hear your Word
Loving Jesus, open our eyes to see your cross
Holy Spirit, open our hearts to receive your gifts
Blessed Trinity, dwell in us and may we dwell in you.

Psalm 30.4–5   **Prayer for the Day**   **Reading:** John 1.29–42

Meditation words: *He brought him to Jesus.*

Lord God,
    we thank you for your apostles
        and especially for Andrew
        who recognized the Messiah
        and, with missionary zeal,
        immediately went for his brother Simon
        and brought him to Jesus.
    So may we become witnesses for you
        bringing men and women to meet with Jesus
        and to accept him as Saviour and Lord.

O Lord our Lord,
    the universe is full of your glory.
    When I look at the sky at night
        and see the stars in their places,
    or by day and see the sun in its beauty
        my heart is filled with praise
        and I know my littleness and worthlessness.
    Yet you, O Lord, have crowned us with honour
        and you have given your Son for our blessing.
    O Lord our Lord, the universe is full of your glory.

Father,
>we praise you for the gift of your Spirit
>>in the life of the world;
>the Spirit brooding upon the waters at creation,
>the Spirit descending as a dove from heaven upon Jesus,
>the Spirit, Christ's gift at Pentecost.
>We praise you Father for your life-giving Spirit
>>in the life and work of the Church.

Response

L: Light of the world, for the joy of answered prayer

R: **We give you thanks and praise.**

Prayer for Peace

>*May you be blessed by the God of Moses*
>>*who witnessed with awe the burning bush*
>*May you be blessed by the God of Moses*
>>*who spoke with courage God's word to Pharaoh*
>*May you be blessed by the God of Moses*
>>*who led his people to the promised land.*

Day 14

May there be silence around us and within us
May the silence be deep and full of meaning
May the silence be profound and healing
May the silence speak to us of God.

Psalm 30.8–12　　**Prayer for the Day**　　**Reading:** John 2.1–11

Meditation words: *This, the first of his miraculous signs, Jesus performed in Cana of Galilee.*

Dear Jesus,
　　you delighted to join the festivities
　　　　when a friend of the family was being married.
　　You did not disdain the lovely joys of human living;
　　　　you entered into the celebration
　　　　with your disciples and your friends.
　　So may we too join the celebration,
　　　　marking the high points of our daily living
　　　　and being ready for the miracles of grace.

　　You are my shepherd, Lord,
　　　　you lead me beside still waters
　　　　　　and bring me to green pastures.
　　When I am low, you restore me.
　　When the shadows are deep, you enlighten me.
　　With you my cup of joy is full
　　　　and I know that in your presence
　　　　　　I shall have goodness and peace
　　　　　　　　all the days of my life.

God of the living Word,
how shall we witness to our faith
amongst the people that are closest to us?
It is not easy to speak of all that matters most
to our family and our neighbours.
Yet this is the most precious gift of all.
Help us to speak to parents, brother, sister,
to neighbours and friends
of the joy that we find in Jesus.

Response

L: Inspire us, Father God, that we might be a people of celebration,

R: Joining with others in songs of joy and peace.

Prayer for Peace

May the sun shed its radiance upon you
May the breezes blow freshly around you
May showers of abundant rain fall upon you
May the Holy Trinity bless you day by day.

Day 15

May the Father surround me with love and care
May the Son speak to me his comforting word
May the Spirit engulf me with creative fire
Blessed Trinity, holy Three, around and within me.

Psalm 31.1–5   **Prayer for the Day**   **Reading:** John 2.13–22

Meditation words: *He . . . drove all from the temple area, both sheep and cattle.*

Lord Jesus,
    help us not to forget
        that at times you showed righteous anger;
    for with the prophet's vigour
        you denounced the commercialization
            of your Father's house of prayer;
        you threw out those who oppressed the needy and the
                        powerless.
    You came with good news for the poor
        and bringing liberation for the oppressed.

Holy God,
    you are my light and my salvation
        so I fear nothing.
    Since you are by my side
        I will not fear if a host should come against me.
    I shall find my joy by dwelling in your house
        and my peace by abiding in your presence.
    Though relatives and friends may forsake me
        yet I know I can put my trust in you.
    Therefore, help me to be strong and courageous
        and to wait upon you, my Father.

Creator God,
>   when people hear your word of grace
>   and come into your house to worship you,
>   they need to find a house of prayer.
>   Deliver us from materialism and greed,
>   deliver us from division and hostility.
>   Enable us as your church
>   that in our life together
>   we may proclaim your love.

Response

L: Great Shepherd, your people cry out in anguish;

R: Grant to the suffering your comfort and strength.

Prayer for Peace

> *May you be blessed with courage like Abraham*
> *   as you take your journey of faith*
> *May you be blessed with vision like Jacob*
> *   when he saw the ladder from earth to heaven*
> *May you be blessed with wisdom like Joseph*
> *   who became a blessing for his people*
> *May you be blessed by God, creator of heaven and earth.*

Day 16

> *Spirit break me, Spirit make me*
> *Spirit mould me, Spirit enfold me*
> *Spirit challenge me, Spirit comfort me*
> *Spirit empty me, Spirit fill me.*

Psalm 31.19–20   **Prayer for the Day**   **Reading:** John 3.1–15

Meditation words: *No one can enter the kingdom of God unless he is born of water and the Spirit.*

Father,
    we are born into the world
        and live through a variety of experiences.
    In the life of the Spirit
      we need to be born again,
        filled with your Spirit of love and power.
    For then we experience variety of gifts
      in the life of your people, the church.

O Lord our God,
    how wonderful it is to hear your voice;
      the voice of the Lord upon the waters
        and in the power of the storm;
      the voice of the Lord in the forests,
        in the cedars and the oak;
      the voice of the Lord in flames of fire
        and in the earthquake;
      the voice of the Lord in the temple
        where all people cry 'Glory',
    May the Lord speak to his people;
    may the Lord bless his people with peace.

Lord God of Abraham, Isaac and Jacob,
  we rejoice that you chose your people
      for special tasks and great responsibilities;
  in the fullness of time amongst the Jews,
      Jesus was born.
  We thank you that you choose your people today
      to proclaim your kingdom to all the nations
  that all the world may know
      Jesus is Lord.

Response

L: Carpenter of Nazareth, creating objects of beauty and
    usefulness

R: Help us to work well in serving others.

Prayer for Peace

> *Let the fire of enthusiasm be in your heart*
> *Let the wisdom of scripture be in your mind*
> *Let the joy of the Spirit be in your life*
> *Let the peace of the Son surround you always*
> *Let the love of the Father enfold you to eternity.*

Day 17

Let the peace of God be woven into our hearts
Let the joy of God be woven into our minds
Let the love of God be woven into our lives
Weaver God, weave your divine pattern into our being.

Psalm 33.1–5   **Prayer for the Day**   **Reading:** John 3.16–21

Meditation words: *God so loved the world that he gave his one and only Son, that whoever believes in him shall not perish but have eternal life.*

Loving God,
 when you desired to show your love
  you held nothing back
  but gave the one most precious to you
  even, Jesus Christ, your Son.
 By his dying and rising again
  he has offered us the gift of life.
 So help us to believe
  that we might enter eternal life.

Friend of the pilgrim way
 when I seek you, you answer me;
  at a time of trouble you reach out to me;
 by your grace and goodness we lack no good thing.
 Help us to depart from evil;
  help us to do good,
   to seek peace and to pursue it.
 You, Lord, redeem the life of your servants;
  help us to take refuge in you
   for with you we find our peace.

Precious Jesus,
    you sent out your disciples
        to proclaim God's kingdom and to heal the sick.
    With that same commission now
        may we too seek to heal the sick and help the needy,
        to proclaim in word and action
        that God's kingdom is here.

Response

L: Give us, Lord, in the place that is home

R: Your peace and your joy.

Prayer for Peace

> *May the song of the nightingale be a blessing to you*
> *May the flight of the dove be a blessing to you*
> *May the song of the lark be a blessing to you*
> *May the great Creator of all living beings*
>   *bless you now and always.*

Day 18

Make your circle around us, Creator God of the winds
Make your circle around us, loving Lord of light
Make your circle around us, holy Spirit of fire
Make your circle around us, blessed Trinity.

Psalm 33.6–9   **Prayer for the Day**   **Reading:** John 3.22–30

Meditation words: *That joy is mine, and it is now complete.*

Creator God,
> in the fullness of time you sent your Son
>> and by your grace you have given witnesses
>> to point to your Son as Saviour.
>
> We give you thanks for John the Baptist
>> whose joy was complete in witnessing to Jesus.
>
> So may we find our happiness in being signposts,
>> pointing to your Son as Saviour.

Lord,
> help us to trust in you and to do good;
>> so shall we live securely.
>
> May we commit our way to you
>> for when we trust you, you will act.
>
> Let us be still before you, Lord,
>> and wait patiently for you.
>
> Keep us from anger, keep us from fretting;
>> but let us wait upon you
>> for then we shall enjoy true prosperity.
>
> You, Lord, love justice and righteousness.
> Help us to keep in your way
>> and to work for justice and for peace;
>
> for the future belongs to the people of peace
>> and all such as put their trust in you.

Living God,
　　you have appointed in the church
　　　　apostles whom you sent to be missionaries
　　　　in Israel and to many nations,
　　　　teaching and baptizing in the name of Jesus.
　　As you sent your apostles long ago
　　　　so send out your messengers today
　　　　to spread the word,
　　　　to build up the church
　　　　and to witness to your Son
　　　　our Saviour Jesus Christ.

Response

L: Steadfast love and faithfulness will meet;

R: **Righteousness and peace will kiss each other.**

Prayer for Peace

May the scent of the rose be a blessing to you
May the sound of the bees be a blessing to you
May the sight of the swallows be a blessing to you
May the voice of God, Father, Son and Spirit, be a blessing to you.

Day 19

I give you my time, Lord, for you give us eternity
I give you my talent, Lord, for you gave us your Son
I give you my love, Lord, for you gave us your Spirit
I give you my self, Lord, for you give us our being.

Psalm 33.12–22   **Prayer for the Day**   **Reading:** John 4.7–30

Meditation words: *Whoever drinks the water I give him will never thirst.*

Eternal source of life,
    around us are the parched deserts of greed
       and the barren wilderness of self-seeking,
    the hot winds of anger
       and the arid fields of passion.
But you have the water of life;
       in you we find the fresh spring of living water.
Bring us to Jesus that we may drink
       and never thirst again.

My soul thirsts for you, Lord God,
    for you, the living God.
I hope in you and praise your name
    for you are my help and my deliverer.
When I pass through the deserts of materialism
       and the wilderness of greed,
       then I long for you
       as a hart longs for flowing streams.

Holy God,
>you have appointed in the church
>>prophets to proclaim the word of the Lord,
>>to warn people on the path of destruction,
>>to encourage people in the way of life,
>>to speak out against the injustice of our time
>>and to stand up for what is good and true.
>So send out your prophets today
>>to witness mightily to your word of truth.

Response

L: Father, when we work for your kingdom

R: **Give us help and guidance through your Holy Spirit.**

Prayer for Peace

>*May the God who divided day from night bless you*
>*May the God who said 'Let there be light' bless you*
>*May the God who divided land from water bless you*
>*May the Creator of the heavens and earth*
>>*bless you now and always.*

Day 20

As the darkness ends, we bow in meditation;
*   as the light breaks, we sing our adoration.*
With the new dawn we voice our praise;
*   in each new day, our song we raise.*
God be with us this and every day;
*   keep us, guide us, in the pilgrim way.*

Psalm 34.4–7   **Prayer for the Day**   **Reading:** John 4.43–54

Meditation words: *He begged him to come and heal his son.*

Father,
   there are times when you are waiting for us to ask;
      simply to have the faith to come to you
      and to give voice to prayer.
   And then you are ready to bless,
      to reach out the hand of healing,
      to restore and to renew.
   As the official long ago came to Jesus,
      so may we in faith come to you
      with our requests for relatives and friends,
      confident in your love, through Jesus Christ our Lord.

Omnipotent God,
   we have heard how you have blessed your people
      in the days of old.
   You have set them free;
      you have driven out their enemies.
   Help us to understand
         that we should not put our trust
            in the bow and the sword,
            in the bomb and the bullet,
         but rather we shall find our security in you.

Keep us faithful to you.
Let us not turn to false gods and idols,
  and in your steadfast love grant us peace and freedom.

God of Eternity,
 you have appointed in your church
  teachers whom you commission to teach your word,
   to build up the church,
   to make known your will to the world.
 Equip through your Holy Spirit
  the teachers in the church today;
  those who teach the children and the young people,
  those who teach the elders and the members,
  those who teach the ministers and missionaries,
   for the equipment of the saints
    and for the glory of your name.

Response

L: May the Lord give strength to his people.

R: May the Lord bless his people with peace.

Prayer for Peace

May God, maker of the great creatures, walk with you
May God, maker of the small creatures, go with you
May God, maker of the sea creatures, speak with you
May God, maker of the birds of the air, hear your prayers
May the God of all living creatures bless you now and always.

Day 21

> *Holy God,*
> > *take the light of my eyes to use in your glory*
> > *take the words of my life to tell out your story*
> > *take the toil of my hands to work in your praise*
> > *take the steps of my feet to walk in your ways.*

Psalm 34.8–10   **Prayer for the Day**   **Reading:** John 5.1–9

Meditation words: *Do you want to get well?*

Lord of the Universe,
> there are times when we need to be challenged
> > and shaken out of our complacency.
> We can become content with our limitations,
> > ready to accept our handicap or illness,
> > > unconcerned about our state of sin.
> Help us to know that we can be forgiven,
> > that there is divine power to heal,
> > > that we can make a new beginning.
> Help us to say 'yes, Lord' when you offer us
> > the healing touch and the word of forgiveness
> > > by the grace of Jesus Christ our Saviour.

Lord God,
> you are our refuge and strength,
> > an ever-present help in trouble.
> So we shall fear nothing
> > though the waters roar and mountains tremble.
> You make wars cease throughout the world;
> > you break the bow and ban the bomb;
> > you shatter the spear
> > and destroy the weapons of mass destruction.
> May the world be still and know that you are God;
> > may we keep silence and know that you are with us;
> > the Lord of hosts, the God of Jacob, you are our refuge.

God of grace,
  you have appointed in the church workers of miracles,
    so that in the story of your people
      prison doors have opened,
      jungles have been penetrated,
      mountains have been scaled
      and parched deserts have become springs of living
                                        water.
  The fury of the persecutor
    has not deterred the mission of the church,
    nor fire, nor bullets, nor shedding of blood.
  By the help of your Spirit the impossible becomes possible;
  miracles abound when we are willing to be co-workers in
                                        your kingdom,
    partners with your Son, our Saviour, Jesus Christ.

Response

L: When the blind man calls out for healing

R: Help us to guide him to the Son of David.

Prayer for Peace

> *May the mystery of the Three surround you*
> *when you rest in the shade of the tree*
> *when you climb to the mountain's crest*
> *when you swim in the ocean's depths*
> *May the mystery of the Three surround you.*

45

Day 22

Father, I offer you my each and every thought
Jesus, I offer you my each and every word
Spirit, I offer you my each and every deed
Holy Trinity, I offer you my being.

Psalm 34.12–14 & 17–18   **Prayer for the Day**

Reading: John 6.1–14 & 35–40

Meditation words: *I am the bread of life. He who comes to me will never go hungry, and he who believes in me will never be thirsty.*

Lord Jesus,
    we live in a world where many people need food
        and many lack pure water to drink.
We rightly work to bring food for the hungry and water for
                         the thirsty
    that they might live healthily.
But there is a deeper hunger and thirst in a land of spiritual
                         need.
For those who seek, you are the bread of life;
    coming to you, people shall find
        that never again will they be hungry or thirsty
    for you satisfy our innermost need.

Loving God,
    how can I be at peace unless I am at one with you,
    and how can I be at one with you
        when my sin stands as a barrier?
Wash me thoroughly from my iniquity;
    wash me that I may be whiter than snow.
Fill me with the joy and gladness
    that come from being forgiven.

The sacrifice you accept is a broken spirit;
    create in me a clean heart, O God,
      and put a new and right spirit within me.
Then shall I be at peace with you and all people.

God, giver of wholeness,
    you have appointed in the church
      healers to be channels of your healing grace,
        going into the world where many suffer from infirmity
                    and disease,
        illnesses of body, mind and spirit.
We thank you for those who by prayer and trust
    bring spiritual healing to your people.
Empower us by the gift of your Spirit
    for this work and witness
      to the glory of your name.

Response

L: O God, you are my God, I seek you.

R: **My soul thirsts for you, as in a dry and weary land where no water is.**

Prayer for Peace

As the rain falls from heaven on the hills
As the streams run down to join the river
As the rivers flow down to join the sea
So may you find blessing in communion with God.

Day 23

Lord, walk with us throughout this day
Lord, speak your word in all we say
Lord, give out your love in our love's endeavour
Lord, express your joy as we abide together.

Psalm 36.5–9   **Prayer for the Day**   **Reading:** John 6.41–65

Meditation words: *Whoever eats my flesh and drinks my blood has eternal life.*

Teacher Jesus,
    it is not easy for us to comprehend
        the deep mysteries which you taught.
When you were teaching on earth
        some disciples left you because they did not understand.
You reminded your other disciples
        that it is the spirit that gives life.
Help us to understand
        that we must spiritually feed upon you
        that we might have eternal life;
grant us that grace and joy
        as we share together in communion here.

Holy God,
    hear me when I call upon you.
There are times when I would like to hide away,
        to shelter like the dove from the raging storm.
Around me in the city I see violence and strife;
        by day and by night there is wrongdoing and trouble,
        there is fraud and oppression of the poor.
But I call upon you and you answer me;
        you give me wisdom and strength
        to proclaim to those in trouble and need.
'Cast your burden upon the Lord
        and he will sustain you.'

Servant Lord,
>you have appointed in the church
>>helpers to enable the work of your people.
>Strengthen those who lead in the worship,
>>those who help to maintain buildings,
>>those who assist in organizations,
>>those who serve amongst the needy in our community.
>Where there are so many practical tasks
>>we thank you for providing the needed helpers.
>Encourage us in the knowledge
>>that we are partners in mission
>>to the glory of your name.

Response

L: Bless the Lord, all his hosts, his ministers that do his will.

R: Bless the Lord, all his works, in all places of his dominion.

Prayer for Peace

>*As the candle burns bright in a dark cave*
>*As the stars cast light on dark streets*
>*As the sun by its dawning scatters the darkness*
>*So may the light of God illumine your life.*

Day 24

Bless our hands, Lord, that they may bless others
Bless our voices, Lord, that they may speak for you
Bless our eyes, Lord, that they may see no evil
Bless our hearts, Lord, that we may seek all good.

Psalm 37.3–7a   **Prayer for the Day**   **Reading:** John 7.37–52

Meditation words: *If anyone is thirsty, let him come to me and drink.*

Saviour Jesus,
    some people seek happiness in wealth or power,
    some in searching out mysteries and deep knowledge,
    some place their trust in law or scour the scriptures;
    but it is only when people come to you
        that they find truth and quench their spiritual thirst.
    Help us to find in you the living fountain
        and to bring others to the same spring of life.

O Lord God,
    for you alone my soul waits in silence;
        from you comes my salvation.
    I may be attacked on all sides;
        enemies may seek to push me over
        as they would a leaning wall.
    But my hope is in you;
            you are my rock and my fortress.
        In you I have my refuge.
    I will trust in you
        for you are the God of power and love.
    For you alone my soul waits in silence.

God of earth and heaven,
>   you have appointed in the church
>>   administrators to enable efficient work for you
>>   and to ensure that everything is done in an orderly way.
>   We ask your guidance for all those
>>   gifted as administrators in the church today;
>>   those responsible for organization and co-ordination,
>>   for communication and publishing,
>>   for buildings and equipment,
>>   for finance and for accounting,
>>   that they may offer this gift
>>   for the work of your kingdom.

Response

L: From the ashes of yesterday's failure

R: **May there grow a new plant of hope.**

Prayer for Peace

May the Father bless you with wisdom in your words
May the Son bless you with compassion in your actions
May the Spirit bless you with joy in your service
May God, Father, Son and Spirit, bless you now and always.

Day 25

> *Be with us Lord as we greet the day*
> *Be with us Lord as we go about our work*
> *Be with us Lord in the eating of our meals*
> *Be with us Lord in the saying of our prayers.*

Psalm 37.25–28 & 30–31   **Prayer for the Day**

Reading: John 8.12–20

Meditation words: *When Jesus spoke again to the people, he said, 'I am the light of the world. Whoever follows me will never walk in darkness, but will have the light of life.'*

Lord God,
    around us is a world of darkness
        and a people struggling to be free.
    You sent Jesus as the light of the world.
    Coming to him we find
        that darkness is overcome
        and life is flooded with light.
    Help us to stand with your Son
        against the forces of darkness
        and to live as children of the light.

O God,
    you are my God,
        I seek you; I thirst for you
        as in a dry land where there is no water;
    And finding you, I know the depth of love
        that is better than life.
    In the holy sanctuary
        I see your power and glory.
    I life up my hands and praise your name.
    When I meditate on you in the quiet of my room
        I sing for joy.

God of the living word,
>> you have appointed in the church
>>> speakers in various kinds of tongues.
>> We give you thanks that there are those
>>> who can praise your holy name
>>> in the spiritual language of Pentecost
>>> or give a message to your people
>>> by your divine inspiration.
>> Guard us from making spiritual gifts
>>> a matter of pride or division.
>> Rather may we share the gifts in love
>>> for the upbuilding of your church.

Response

L: Keep me as the apple of your eye;

R: **Hide me in the shadow of your wings.**

Prayer for Peace

May the Father inspire you with the gift of love
May the Son enliven you with the gift of joy
May the Spirit enfold you with the gift of peace
May God, Father, Son and Spirit, abide with you always.

Day 26

Father, guide us in our journeys
Jesus, bless us in our travels
Spirit, go with us on our pilgrimage
Holy God, blessed Three,
  be with us where we go and where we stay.

Psalm 39.4–6   **Prayer for the Day**   **Reading:** John 8.21–38

Meditation words: *You will know the truth, and the truth will set you free.*

Risen Jesus,
  we search for meaning in life;
  we quest after the philosopher's stone;
  we come to you and find the truth,
    truth that frees us from prejudice,
    that breaks the bonds of sin
    and opens the way ahead.

Lord God,
  may the kings of the nations
    seek justice for the poor
    and defend their cause.
  In the days of our Queen
    may righteousness flourish and peace abound.
  You, Lord, have pity for the weak and needy,
    you protect them from violence and oppression.
  So lead us in the ways of justice and of peace
    that our rulers and our people may live in your praise.

God of grace,
>your gifts to the church
>>were that some in the church should be pastors
>>who care for your people,
>>guiding them when perplexed,
>>comforting them in sorrow,
>>encouraging them in faith
>>and sharing their joys.
>We thank you for your pastors today
>>and pray that you will grant them
>>the gift of your Holy Spirit
>>to enable them for their work and witness.

Response

L: Father, guide us in the pilgrimage of life

R: **That we may bear one anothers' burdens and share each others' joys.**

Prayer for Peace

May the Father grant you the gift of patience
May the Son grant you the gift of kindness
May the Spirit grant you the gift of goodness
May God, Father, Son and Spirit, bless you day by day.

Day 27

May the deep peace of God be in our hearts
May the deep peace of the Son be in our lives
May the deep peace of the Spirit be amongst us
May we share the peace of the Trinity with all around us.

Psalm 40.1–3   **Prayer for the Day**   **Reading:** John 8.39–59

Meditation words: '*I tell you the truth,*' *Jesus answered,* '*before Abraham was born, I am!*'

Eternal God,
    we praise you that you are the creator of the universe,
        the beginning and the end,
        for before time was, you are.
    We praise you that you are one with the Son
        who existed before all time
        yet came into time
        that by timely and perfect sacrifice
        he might offer us eternal life,
        the bliss of your presence beyond time
        that we might praise you in eternity.

O Lord of hosts,
    how lovely is your house.
    I long to be in your sanctuary.
    My heart sings for joy in worship of you,
        the living God.
    In your house, together with your people,
        I find deep peace and lasting joy.
    A day in your house is better
        than a thousand anywhere else,
        for you, Father, are a blazing sun
        blessing us in the brightness of your light.

Holy Spirit,
    your gifts were that some in the church should be evangelists
        who go from village to village,
            from city to city, from country to country,
                proclaiming the good news of your kingdom.
    We give you thanks for evangelists today
        who proclaim the name of Jesus as Saviour and Lord
        and pray that you will enable them
            by your spiritual gifts
        to be faithful ambassadors
            of the gospel of Jesus Christ.

Response

L: Lord, you call your people in every place to proclaim the good news of salvation.

R: **Give us joy in our partnership in mission.**

Prayer for Peace

May the Father bless you with the gift of faithfulness
May the Son inspire in you the quality of gentleness
May the Spirit enable you to exercise self-control
May God, Father, Son and Spirit, bless you this day and always.

Day 28

I seek my peace in you, Lord
I seek my peace in you
I find my joy in you, Lord
I find my joy in you
I give my love to you, Lord
I give my love to you.

Psalm 40.9–11   **Prayer for the Day**   **Reading:** John 9.1–41

Meditation words: *One thing I do know. I was blind but now I see!*

Father God,
    your Son does such wonderful things;
    he transforms life for us
        if we are ready to trust him.
    There are those who try to make us betray him
        but we know from experience
        that Jesus is the man of love
        who brings us abundant blessings.
    Before we met Jesus and gave ourselves to him
        we were blind to so much in life;
        now we see.

God our Lord,
    help us to listen to your voice
        for you speak peace to your people.
    Your salvation is near
        for those who obey and trust you.
    When we do so there is glory in the Lord;
        love and faith rest together,
        righteousness and peace kiss each other.

So turn us to you, O Lord,
>   make us a people of peace
>   that we may receive from you
>   all that is good.

Lord Jesus,
>   you are our peace;
>   you have broken down the dividing wall of hostility;
>   you have made peace through the blood of your cross,
>   giving yourself that we might be one with the Father.
>   You preached peace to those far away
>   and peace to those near at hand
>   so that people near and far
>   might be made one with each other
>   and find peace with God.

Response

L: When we are surrounded by the dark

R: Jesus is the light of life.

Prayer for Peace

May God the great Spirit accompany your journeying
May God the Mother of all being watch over your progress
May God the spark of all life ignite your enthusiasm
May the triune God, the great mystery, give you a benediction.

Day 29

The peace of the Father is with us
The peace of the Son is here
The peace of the Spirit is with us
The peace of the Three is here.

Psalm 42.1–5   Prayer for the Day   Reading: John 10.1–10

Meditation words: *Jesus said again, 'I tell you the truth, I am the gate for the sheep ... whoever enters through me will be saved.'*

Lord Jesus,
    you know your people
        as the shepherd knows the sheep.
    You preserve us from danger
        for you keep the door of the fold.
    When we come to you and put our trust in you
        then we find eternal life,
            the salvation you alone can give.

Lord most high,
    let me dwell in your shadow
        for you are my refuge and fortress.
    You deliver me from the snare of the fowler
        and the traps laid by my enemies.
    In your presence we do not fear the terror by night
        nor attacks by day,
    not the pestilence of darkness
        nor the wasting disease of noonday.
    Though a thousand people fall
        we will find safety if we put our trust in you,
            the Most High God.
    For you will bear us up
        and hold us in your arms.

We are bound together in love
and you are our salvation.

Divine Father,
every family in heaven and on earth is named after you.
According to the riches of your glory
grant that we may be strengthened with might
in our inward being by your Spirit.
May Christ dwell in our hearts through faith
so that we, rooted and grounded in love,
may have power to comprehend with the saints
the breadth, length, height and depth
of your love in Christ Jesus
and that we may be filled with your fullness.

Response

L: Some trust in chariots and some in horses,

R: But we trust in the name of the Lord our God.

Prayer for Peace

The God of yesterday has done great things for you
The God of today shows great signs for you
The God of tomorrow will perform great wonders for you
The God of eternity, Father, Son and Spirit,
bless you now and always.

> *In the stillness we worship God*
> *In the quiet we know his presence*
> *His peace passes our understanding*
> *In the stillness we worship God.*

Psalm 46.1–3   **Prayer for the Day**   **Reading:** John 10.11–18

Meditation words: *I am the good shepherd; I know my sheep and my sheep know me.*

Dearest Jesus,
>   how much you care for your people.
>> When we are lost, you search us out;
>> when we are sick, you heal us;
>> when we are perplexed, you guide us;
>> when we are sorrowful, you comfort us.
>   You know us better than we know ourselves.
>   We know you and we delight to hear your voice.
>   Make us ready when you call
>> to respond by following you.

Lord,
>   it is good to sing your praise
>> and to declare your unfailing love by day and night.
>   We shall celebrate with organ and guitar,
>> with drums and cymbals,
>   for you have made us glad
>> and filled our hearts with joy.
>   You call us to your service
>> both in youth and in old age;
>   when we are faithful to you
>> you pour upon us the fresh oil of peace.

We have a gospel to proclaim;
    it is the gospel of peace.
Knowing that we are engaged in spiritual conflict, Lord,
    we put on the breastplate of righteousness,
    on our feet the equipment of the gospel of peace,
    and take the shield of faith.
With all the spiritual armour you give us, Father,
    we are ready for the conflict
        with spiritual hosts of wickedness.
Be at our side
    that we may remain faithful in the struggle.

Response

L: Unless the Lord builds the house

R: Those who build it labour in vain.

Prayer for Peace

May you find deep stillness in your ocean journey
May you find deep quiet on the high mountain
May you find the inward silence of mystic contemplation
May the peace of the Blessed Trinity
    be yours to your life's fulfilment.

Day 31

Take away from me all anxieties
Remove from me all my cares
Help me to relax in your divine presence
Come, Holy Spirit, give us your peace.

Psalm 46.4–7   Prayer for the Day   Reading: John 11.1–27

Meditation words: *Jesus said to her, 'I am the resurrection and the life. He who believes in me will live, even though he dies; and whoever lives and believes in me will never die.'*

Precious Jesus,
    when you came to the friends you loved
        there was sorrow in the house for the loss of Lazarus.
You spoke the word of love and Lazarus rose
        and there was a song of celebration.
So too today you speak to us in times of despair and sorrow;
        the pain goes and we celebrate together.
We may not always find the miracle of resurrection
        to restore the ones we love
but we always find the miracle of love
        and the compassion of your voice.
Help us, dear Lord, to find our joy in you.

We bless your name, O Lord,
    and remember all your benefits,
    for you forgive our sins,
    you heal our diseases,
    you redeem us from destruction,
    you crown us with love and mercy,
    you renew our youth like the eagles,
    you make our lives wholesome and good.
You bring justice for the oppressed,
    you are merciful to those who err.

As far as the east is from the west
so far do you remove our sin from us.
We bless your name, O Lord,
for your love which is from everlasting to everlasting.

Saviour Jesus,
you commissioned your people
to go into all the world,
making disciples, teaching and baptizing.
Inspire us in your name to go out
preaching the good news of your salvation.

Response

L: Lord, when fear and darkness threaten to overwhelm us

R: **May your love cast out the fear and your light banish the dark.**

Prayer for Peace

May the God of the changing seasons bless your years
May the God of all living creatures bless your journeys
May the God of sun, moon and stars bless your meditation
May God, Father, Son and Holy Spirit, bless you in discipleship.

Day 32

Weave your name O God into my mind
Weave your power O God into my life
Weave your love O God into my heart
Weaver God, may the warp and woof of your divine nature
  pattern my life for your glory.

Psalm 46.8–11   **Prayer for the Day**   **Reading: John 12.1–8**

Meditation words: *Mary took about a pint of pure nard, an expensive perfume; she poured it on Jesus' feet.*

Crucified Jesus,
  we give you thanks for Mary
    who was willing to make a costly gift
    to anoint your feet and show her love.
  There are times when we need to make our costly sacrifice,
    to show that we put you above all things
    in our love and in our lives.
  Since you gave so much for us
    anything we give is but a small return.
  Help us to offer you our lives
    in joyful dedication and glad thanksgiving.

O Lord my God,
  you are very great.
  You stretch out the heavens like a tent;
  you set the earth on its foundations;
  you make springs gush in the valleys;
  you cause grass to grow for the animals.
  You bring forth food from the earth
    and give joy to your people with wine and oil.
  We all look to you
    and you give us food in each season.

You open your hand and bless us abundantly
and grant us the gift of your Spirit
to renew and recreate us.
O Lord my God, you are very great.

Dear Jesus,
I walk through the city and see a thousand joyless faces.
I travel on the trains and see a multitude unsmiling.
In the city squares people mill about
and crowd into the shops and supermarkets.
They are like sheep without a shepherd.
How they need to hear your voice.
Help us, Lord, to speak for you and call them to your side.

Response

L: Father, when our pilgrimage of faith calls for sacrifice

R: **Help us not to count the cost, but to offer all to you.**

Prayer for Peace

May the God of earthquake, wind and fire inspire you
May the God of the still small voice speak to you
May the God of mystic communion be one with you
May God, Father, Son and Spirit,
be with you to your journey's end.

Day 33

In the stillness of the morning
In the quiet of the day
In the stillness of the evening
I hear the voice of God and my heart rejoices.

Psalm 47   **Prayer for the Day**   **Reading:** John 12.20–26

Meditation words: *I tell you the truth, unless a grain of wheat falls to the ground and dies, it remains only a single seed. But if it dies, it produces many seeds.*

Redeemer Jesus,
    when we cling to life's pleasures and are not prepared for
                                            sacrifice
        then life becomes empty and barren.
    But when we are ready to die to self and to offer all to you,
        then we become all that we were meant to be
        and we bear fruit in your kingdom.
    So make us like that grain of wheat,
        sown small, lost in the ground,
        but bearing a mighty crop for you.

God of travellers
    we give you thanks for you are good.
    You satisfy the thirsty and fill the hungry;
        you heal the sick who call upon you;
        you are with those who sail the seas.
    When the storm winds blow and the waves rise
        and your people call to you in distress
        you still the storm and hush the waves.
    You bring your people to the haven of peace;
        you turn the desert into pools of water
            and give a fruitful yield in the fields.

You raise up the needy and feed the hungry
    so that all the families of the earth
        know your unfailing love.
O Lord our God, we give you thanks.

God of mercy
    there are times when we seek signs
        and need reassurance of your purpose and your love.
We thank you that in the abundance of your grace
        you grant us signs from time to time,
        to strengthen our resolve, deepen our faith
        and encourage us in the pilgrim way.

Response

L: May the Lord give strength to his people!

R: May the Lord bless his people with peace!

Prayer for Peace

As the sun in its shining brings glory
As the stars in the night scatter dark
As the moon gives us hope in its radiance
So may the light of God
    fill your heart and your mind and your life.

Day 34

We come apart from bustle and noise
We turn aside from clamour and anxiety
We seek our peace in the heart of God
We find our peace, we find our peace with you Lord.

Psalm 48.1–3   **Prayer for the Day**   **Reading:** John 12.27–36

Meditation words: *I, when I am lifted up from the earth, will draw all men to myself.*

Crucified Jesus,
> you gave yourself for your people
> > being lifted up on the cross
> > that we might be lifted up in glory.
> You were ready to sacrifice yourself
> > that your people might walk in the light.
> Deliver us from darkness
> > that we might be children of light.
> Draw us to yourself
> > as you draw all people by your love.

Giver of Life,
> your word is a lamp to my feet and a light to my path.
> I love your commandments more than gold;
> > yes, even the finest gold.
> I rise before dawn and cry to you for help
> > and in the evening I meditate on your word.
> In you I find my hope
> > and you show me steadfast love.
> Throughout the day I praise your name
> > and I find joy in your word.
> To those who love your law
> > you give great peace.

Risen Jesus,
    for long your church has served you
        through times of testing and difficulty,
        facing indifference and hostility.
    But now new days have come;
        the Spirit is moving mightily
        and men and women are turning to you in faith.
    We thank you that in the arid deserts of materialism
        you have given us showers of blessing
        and poured out spiritual gifts for your people.
    Keep us responsive in proclaiming your word
        and serving your people.

Response

L: I love the house where you live, O Lord,

R: **The place where your glory dwells.**

Prayer for Peace

May the maker of light give light to your eyes
May the restorer of sight give sight to your eyes
May the guide of the inward seeing give depth to your eyes
May Father, Son and Spirit be in your seeing and being.

Day 35

Creator God,
>Thou art the peace of the dove's flight
>Thou art the joy of the lark's song
>Thou art the grace of the deer's run
>Thou art the love of mother for son.

Psalm 50.1–4   **Prayer for the Day**   **Reading:** John 13.1–15

Meditation words: *After that he poured water into a basin and began to wash his disciples' feet.*

Servant Jesus,
>what love you showed to your disciples
>>and what humility in your service.
>You are the Lord of life, Son of God,
>>yet you stooped down
>>to take off the grimy sandals
>>and to wash their dusty feet.
>With loving care you dried them with the towel
>>making them fresh and cool.
>Since you, our Lord and Saviour,
>>did such lowly service for us,
>>ought we not humbly to serve others also?

Lord God,
>it is not easy to walk in your way
>>when we seek peace among the nations.
>We find there are many who hate peace
>>and prefer to seek the victory in war.
>Even amongst our neighbours and friends
>>are those who want to prepare for war.
>I am for peace;
>>but when I speak, they are for war.

In my distress I call to you, O Lord;
give me the courage and the faith
to speak for peace.

Spirit of God
you call your people to patient endurance
that we might not fail in time of testing,
that we might not grow weary in well-doing,
that we should not abandon our first love.
Help us to find our constant inspiration in you
that the lamp may be kept burning
as we witness by your grace.

Response

L: I am still confident of this: I will see the goodness of the Lord in the land of the living.

R: **Wait for the Lord; be strong and take heart and wait for the Lord.**

Prayer for Peace

The maker of the silver fish, cascading shoal, be near you
The maker of the great fish, white whale, be around you
The maker of the gentle fish, playful dolphin, be close to you
May the Great Lord of sea creatures swim with you.

Day 36

In the heart of the leaf, veins
In the flat of the palms, veins
Through the veins, life blood
Drawn from heart or roots, sustenance
Given from the source of all creation
Life blood, life food.

Psalm 52.8–9   **Prayer for the Day**   **Reading:** John 13.21–30

Meditation words: *I tell you the truth, one of you is going to betray me.*

Crucified Saviour,
    Forgive us for those times when we have denied you.
    Guard us from the temptation
        to betray you in thought, word or action.
    You grieved deeply for Judas
        who brought darkness into his life by betrayal.
    You long to draw your people to yourself,
           to guide us away from the path of darkness,
      and you are always ready to forgive.
    Help us to remain faithful to you,
        to resist temptation
    and to seek the help of the Holy Spirit
        in doing your will to the glory of God our Creator.

I am glad when I go to worship
    in the cathedral in the heart of our city.
Jerusalem was built as a city bound firmly together,
    to which all the people journeyed.
We pray for the peace of the city.
May peace be within its walls
    and security in all its houses.
In our city, in your city, in the divided cities of our world,

for the sake of fellow citizens I pray
   'Peace be within you.'
In the name of God
   we will seek good for the city.

Living God,
   it pleases you when your people are known
      by their works, their love, their faith,
      their service and their patient endurance.
   Help us to live by your power
      that we may receive the morning star
      and shine in your reflected light.

Response

L: Lord, when the storms of conflict and doubt rage around us

R: **Your word gives us purpose and peace.**

Prayer for Peace

May your feet walk in the way of the Lord
May your voice speak the word of the Lord
May your hands serve God in blessing others
May your life show something of the glory of God
May you know the peace of God now and always.

Day 37

God is praised by the whole of creation
> *By the tiniest plant drawing sustenance from earth*
> *By the smallest leaf drawing energy from the sun*
> *By the most minute tendril passing moisture to the fruit*
>> *God's name is praised.*

Psalm 53.1–2 & 6 **Prayer for the Day** **Reading:** John 13.31–38

Meditation words: *A new command I give you: Love one another. As I have loved you, so you must love one another.*

Redeemer Jesus,
> your whole life was an expression of love,
>> your teaching, your healing, your being.
> You gave what was precious to redeem those you loved.
> And to each person whose life you bought
>> you gave this new command,
>> to love as you have loved,
>> to love one another, deeply, sacrificially.
> Root us in the soil of your love
>> that we may bear fruit for your kingdom.

When men rise up against us,
> when the enemy is at our gates,
> when nations come in anger against us,
>> it is easy to give way to fear
>>> and to seek our security in weapons of war.
> But when we trust you, Lord,
>> we escape as a bird from the fowler's snare.
> When you are on our side
>> none can have the victory over us.
> Let us find our help in you,
>> O Lord God, creator of heaven and earth.

Enlivening God,
    we know that in your church
        we are sometimes as those who sleep
        or even as those who want to be known as lively
        but appear as those who are dead.
    Revive your church, O Lord,
        awaken us and strengthen us.
    Help us to repent and to begin again
        with new life and new hope.
    Empower us by your Holy Spirit
        to do your will and to proclaim your love
        and may our names be written in the book of life.

Response

L: Lord, when the testing times of persecution come

R: **Give to your saints courage, faith and hope.**

Prayer for Peace

May the Lord of the silver moon shine upon you
May the King of the myriad stars reign over you
May the Maker of the bright sun shed warmth around you
May the living Centre of the great Universe draw you to himself.

Day 38

> *Amethyst, blue as the colour of the ocean*
> *Emerald, green as the grass in the fields*
> *Garnet, red as blood freely shed*
> *Gems of the earth, precious,*
> > *but not as precious as the love of God in Christ.'*

Psalm 55.16–17 & 22   **Prayer for the Day**   **Reading:** John 14.1–7

Meditation words: *Jesus answered, 'I am the way and the truth and the life. No one comes to the Father except through me.'*

Father God,
>   so many people feel lost in life
>   and they long to find a way through.
>   Jesus is the way to happiness, to fulfilment and to meaning.
>   Lead us in your way.
Father, so many people long to know the truth
>   and they search ancient teachings.
>   Jesus is the truth they seek, the key to knowledge and to
>   understanding.
>   Teach us your truth.
Lord God, so many people need life;
>   they exist in sleep or on the verge of death.
>   Jesus is the life, abundant life, creative life.
>   Help us to live in Christ that he may live in us.

When you bless the nations with good, O Lord,
>   we are like those who dream;
our hearts are filled with joy
>   and our lives transformed with laughter.
The Lord has done great things for us, we say,
>   and we join in celebration.
You have blessed us abundantly, Lord God.

Though we have had a seedtime of tears
    you have given us a harvest in joy.
So let us put our trust in you
    that we may reap an abundant harvest
        with a glad and happy celebration.

God of grace,
    you have set before us an open door;
        help us to go through and to keep your word.
We lack power when we act in our own strength
    but you enable us by your mighty power.
Help us to endure in times of trial;
    make us to be pillars in your temple
        and to hold fast that which is good.
So may we come at the last to the new Jerusalem,
    the city of our God.

Response

L: Lord God, in those times when I feel lost

R: Guide me to Jesus, the way of life.

Prayer for Peace

May the God of travellers be with you as you journey
May the Christ of the pilgrim way walk alongside you
May the Spirit of light illumine your path
Go well and the God of peace go with you.

Day 39

> *May you know the blessing of rain from heaven*
> *May the furrows of the fields be full of water*
> *May the streams of the land never run dry*
> *May the rivers flow majestically to the sea.*

Psalm 56.10–13   Prayer for the Day   Reading: John 14.8–14

Meditation words: *I tell you the truth, anyone who has faith in me will also do what I have been doing. He will do even greater things than these, because I am going to the Father.*

Risen Jesus,
>　how wonderful are your promises to us.
>　You made such an impact in the lives of people around you;
>　　you healed, helped and encouraged.
>　Yet you also inspire us to do your work
>　　and promise that in your name
>　　we shall do even greater things.
>　What a responsibility you gave us;
>　　what a challenge in discipleship.
>　Lord, keep us faithful
>　　in all that you have entrusted to us.

Lord our God,
>　unless you bless the building of our house
>　　we build in vain;
>　unless you watch over our city
>　　all our defences are useless.
>　You are our true security;
>　　when we trust you, we sleep soundly.
>　Lord God, may we find our peace in doing your will,
>　　for then we shall find blessings
>　　　both today and tomorrow.

Holy Spirit,
> we do not please you
>> when we are uncommitted and half-hearted,
>> when we are neither hot nor cold.
> Forgive us.
>> We say we are rich when we are truly poor;
>> we say that we see clearly when we are blind.
> Help us to buy gold refined by fire
>> and to have our eyes opened to you.
> When Jesus stands at the door and knocks
>> may we be ready to open and to welcome him.

Response

L: Lord, when the way of service and witness is hard

R: Help us to put our trust in your promises.

Prayer for Peace

> *May the Creator God encircle you with his love*
> *May Jesus our Lord encircle you with his joy*
> *May the Holy Spirit encircle you with his peace*
> *May the blessed Trinity fill you with hope and faith.*

Day 40

> *May the wind in your face refresh you*
> *May the sun overhead warm you*
> *May the stars at night guide you*
> *May the clouds in the sky be signs of God's glory.*

Psalm 57.1–3   **Prayer for the Day**   **Reading:** John 14.15–24

Meditation words: *I will ask the Father, and he will give you another Counsellor to be with you for ever – the Spirit of truth.*

Lord Jesus,
    we give thanks for your gift to the church,
        the Holy Spirit, our Counsellor.
    By his guidance we are led into truth;
        in his power we can do your will;
        by his inspiration we proclaim your gospel.
    So from the Father through the Son
        we receive the Holy Spirit.
    To you be the praise, One God,
        Father, Son and Spirit for ever and ever.

Father,
    when we walk in your way
        then we know the secret of true happiness;
        we know the delight of work well done;
        we experience joy in family life
            and the blessing of an open table.
    May we delight to see peace and prosperity in our city;
    may we be blessed in future generations;
    may there be peace in our nation and peace in our world.
    May God grant us prosperity all the days of our life.

Living God,
you have given us a vision
of a new heaven and a new earth,
of the holy city, new Jerusalem.
Enable us by your Holy Spirit
to go into the cities today
to share that vision and proclaim your name.
To the depressed and the despairing,
to the poor and the homeless,
may we give the good news
that your home, Father, is with humankind,
that you will live with us
and we shall be your people.

Response

L: Holy Spirit, without your aid we are weak and anxious;

R: Grant us your gifts of wisdom, power and peace.

Prayer for Peace

May your rising be as the lark for happiness
May your working be as the ox with contentment
May your resting be as the dove for peace
May your days and nights be surrounded by God's splendour.

Day 41

Grass bending with the strength of the wind
Trees leaning over before the gale
Clouds scudding across the sky before the force of the storm
God of creation, Lord of the skies, be with us.

Psalm 57.7–11   **Prayer for the Day**   **Reading:** John 14.25–31

Meditation words: *Peace I leave with you; my peace I give you.*
I do not give to you as the world gives.

God of harmony,
    when the nations seek peace
        they make their treaties and alliances.
    There is peace of a kind
        but it is subject to betrayals and denials;
        there is still a lack of brotherhood and love.
    But your peace goes deeper.
    Your peace draws people together with their neighbours.
    Your peace makes us one with you.
    Your peace is sacrificial love
        which recognizes the good in all people,
        stands out against injustice and oppression
        and frees people to realize their full potential.
    Your peace is health and holiness,
        it is wholeness and salvation.
    May we find our peace through Christ.

Lord,
    teach me humility
        that I may not make great claims or proud boasts.
    I have become calm and quiet,
        like a child quieted by its mother.
    So I put my hope in you
        and in you I find my peace.

Holy God,
    you have shown us the river of the water of life,
        bright as crystal, flowing from your throne,
    and the tree of life
        with its leaves for the healing of nations.
    Send us out to the nations of the world
        proclaiming the Lamb, Jesus our Lord,
        that your people may worship you
        and may welcome you as the light in our midst
        for ever and ever.

Response

L: Father, you are the God of the oppressed;

R: Hear and bless your suffering children.

Prayer for Peace

May the Father who loves you bless you
May the Son who redeems you bless you
May the Spirit who enables you bless you
May the Holy Trinity bless you this and every day.

Day 42

The flower bursts through hard ground to grow towards the
*   light*
The wheat grows steadily towards the warming sun
The tree reaches its branches ever higher towards the sky
So in our life of prayer we stretch expectantly up towards God.

Psalm 59.9 & 16–17 **Prayer for the Day** **Reading:** John 15.1–4

Meditation words: *I am the true vine, and my Father is the gardener. He cuts off every branch in me that bears no fruit, while every branch that does bear fruit he prunes so that it will be even more fruitful.*

Dear Jesus,
    we praise you for you are the vine,
        fruitful for the Father, full of blessing.
    We thank you that you enable us to grow in you,
        fruitful for the kingdom.
    Help us to guard against being barren vines,
        to be cut away and burned.
    Discipline us; prune us; take away what is bad
        that we may bear more fruit yet
        and may live to the glory of God, our Father.

O Lord my God,
    you have searched me and known me.
    You go before me and know all my ways.
    Where shall I go from your Spirit?
        How can I hide from your presence?
    If I should take the wings of the morning
        and go to the furthest parts of the sea,
            even there you would find me out.

Even if I should try to hide in darkness
   I find with you that night is bright as day.
You formed me in my mother's womb
   and I am wonderfully and mysteriously made.
Search me, O God, and know my heart
   and may I find in you the way to peace.

Jesus,
   you are the son of David,
      the bright morning star,
      the beginning and the end,
      the first and the last.
   Help us to proclaim the good news to those who are thirsty
      that they will find in you the water of life, without price.

Response

L: Lord God, rebuke us, discipline us, guide us,

R: That we may be fruitful vines in the garden of your kingdom.

Prayer for Peace

   Go into the world to speak with courage
   Go into the world to act with compassion
   Go into the world to encourage your neighbours
   Go into the world to witness to the gospel
   And may the blessed Trinity, Father, Son and Spirit,
      inform and inspire your thinking, speaking and action.

Day 43

Brown twigs are clothed with light green leaves; it is spring
Light green changes to deep green; it is summer
Green turns to golden brown; it is autumn
Leaves fall, the branches are bare; it is winter
Through all the changing seasons
God's sap of life flows through us.

Psalm 61.1–4   **Prayer for the Day**   **Reading:** John 15.5–9

Meditation words: *If a man remains in me and I in him, he will bear much fruit; apart from me you can do nothing.*

Loving Father,
   you sent your Son, our Saviour Jesus Christ,
      that we might live in him and he in us.
   For in such abiding
      we can bear fruit for your kingdom.
   Cut off from him, we wither and die
      like a plant in the desert.
   Without the help and inspiration of your Son
      we are weak and powerless.
   But abiding in Jesus our Lord
      we can achieve great things
      and become fruitful vines for you.

O Lord our God,
   we sing your praises for it is good and right to do so.
   You heal the downcast and bind their wounds.
   Your power is abundant and your love beyond measure.
   You lift up the oppressed and you rebuke the wicked.

O Lord our God, we sing your praise
   for you are the security of our city;
   you bless our children, you make peace in our country,
   you give us a fine harvest,
   you declare your good news to your people.
O Lord our God, we sing your praise.

God of peace,
   amongst the nations there is war;
   between the people, there is division;
   within each person is an inner struggle.
   So throughout the world
      your people cry out for reconciliation,
      for your great salvation.
   Help us so to proclaim the glad news of deliverance
      that people may find a new meaning in life
      as they give themselves to you.

Response

L: Father, make us one with you,

R: One with your Son and one in your Spirit.

Prayer for Peace

May God be with you in the saying of your prayers
May God be with you in the doing of your work
May God be with you in all your time of leisure
May God's light illumine all your pilgrim way.

Day 44

The soil, rich in texture, holding water, sustains the roots
The roots, reaching out, drawing food and drink, sustain the stem
The stem, drawing from the roots, sustains the branches
The whole plant, root, stem and branches,
  gives glory to God the Creator.

Psalm 62.1–2 & 5–8   **Prayer for the Day**

Reading: John 15.10–17

Meditation words: *I have told you this so that my joy may be in you and that your joy may be complete.*

You have filled our lives with joy, dear Jesus,
  and that joy is of surpassing worth.
Our lives are a celebration of all your gifts and your love.
Your teaching is our constant inspiration;
  your promises are our delight;
  in your word to us we have the joy that overflows,
  abundant joy from the Lord of love.

Praise the Lord.
We give you praise, Father God, in your church,
  praising you for the beauty of nature,
  for all your wonderful acts
    and for the exceeding greatness of your being.
We praise you with the trumpet,
  with lute and harp, timbrel and dance,
  with strings and pipe and clashing cymbals.
Let every living being praise your name.
Praise the Lord.

Living Jesus,
    you sent your disciples on mission two by two,
        to proclaim your gospel.
    So send us out to do your work,
        staying with Christian friends,
        available for the work of your kingdom,
        telling out the good news of your love.

Response

L: Father, you have filled our lives with love and light.

R: **Help us to be signs of joy and instruments of peace.**

Prayer for Peace

May the Father go with you on your journey of discovery
May the Son be your companion on your pilgrim way
May the Spirit be your guide in your quest for truth
May the blessed Trinity be with you by day and by night.

Day 45

Grey-black clouds, seemingly menacing yet full of promise
Life-giving rain, falling as a curtain from the sky
Streams and rivulets run into rivers
  and the rivers flow majestically down to the sea.
See the gift of God in the water of life.

Psalm 62.9–12 **Prayer for the Day** **Reading:** John 15.17–25

Meditation words: *Remember the words that I spoke to you: 'No servant is greater than his master.' If they persecuted me, they will persecute you also.*

Shepherd Jesus,
  you came into the world to save the lost
    and to show love to all people;
      yet you were persecuted, tortured and killed.
  You call your people to preach your word
    and to live the life of love and sharing.
  The world rejects such teaching and such action
    and persecutes your people too.
  Forgive them and keep us faithful
    that in spite of opposition and suffering
    we may proclaim your message to the world.

God of grace,
  when trenches are dug between armies,
  when barriers are raised in cities,
  when walls divide communities,
  when bullets maim and kill,
  when bombs destroy and obliterate,
  then we need the reconciling message of your Son
    and the transforming peace of your Spirit.

God of love,
>   there are times in the life of the church
>>   and of each one of us
>   that we go astray and betray you.
>   Forgive us all the faults of the past.
>   Forgive us for faithlessness, selfishness,
>>   for immorality and idolatry.
>   Help us to know that forgiven we are free
>>   and can make a new beginning;
>   help us to proclaim your love
>>   which forgives again and again.

Response

L: Lord, you have blessed us in the morning of life;

R: Keep us faithful to you in the evening of our years.

Prayer for Peace

> *May the peace of the rivers be in your heart*
> *May the peace of the trees be in your life*
> *May the peace of the stars be in your soul*
> *Peace of the Great Spirit to you and yours.*

Day 46

*We welcome the dawn, the sun rising glorious to announce a new
    day
We rejoice in the noonday, the blessing of work and of leisure
We are content at sunset, heralding a welcome time of rest
God of day and night, be with us in our working and sleeping.*

Psalm 63.1–5   **Prayer for the Day**   **Reading:** John 15.26–16.4

Meditation words: *When the Counsellor comes, whom I will
send to you from the Father, the Spirit of truth who goes out from
the Father, he will testify about me.*

Dear Jesus,
    your promises are precious to us
        and amongst them this promise of the Counsellor.
    The Spirit of truth who comes from the Father,
        your gift to the church,
    is comfort in times of persecution
        and challenge in times of ease.
    Send us out as your witnesses
        empowered by the Holy Spirit,
            the great witness to all things good.

Shepherd Jesus,
    help us to live in peace,
        agreeing with one another
        instead of splitting our family by arguments,
        dividing the church by disagreements
        and weakening our community by constant quarrels.
    By mutual understanding and taking time to care
        help us to live at peace
        and, in our midst, to know the God of love and peace.

God of grace,
    when your children wander from you,
    when they waste their lives in selfishness,
    when they show pride and passion,
        greed and temper, lust for power,
    you do not reject them
        but forgiving always, you offer them your love.
    Help us, O Lord, to accept your love
        and to declare it to the world.

Response

L: Lord God, when we become dispirited or disillusioned

R: Grant us renewal through your Holy Spirit.

Prayer for Peace

God be with you in your greeting of the day
God be with you in the work you undertake
God be with you in your worship of his name
God be with you in your resting through the night.

Day 47

Cry of birds, calling high on the mountain
Sound of sea creatures, deep in the ocean
Lowing of cattle, out in the fields
Sound of God's voice, calling to heart and mind.

Psalm 65.1–4   **Prayer for the Day**   **Reading:** John 16.5–15

Meditation words: *It is for your good that I am going away. Unless I go away, the Counsellor will not come to you; but if I go, I will send him to you.*

Redeemer Jesus,
    you were so open and honest,
        so comforting and challenging,
    when you taught your disciples.
Who could expect that anything could compensate
    for your leaving them?
But you were careful of their welfare
    and knew the difference that the Holy Spirit would
                make.

At Pentecost your promise was fulfilled.
As the lives of your disciples were transformed
      by the gift of the Spirit
    so may we be enlivened and enabled
      by your spiritual gifts.

Creator Spirit,
    how can we proclaim peace to the world
      if we do not show peace within ourselves?
Help us to share peace with the people around us
    and to express love with faith.
Fill our lives
      that we might live to the glory of the Father
        through the inspiration of our Lord Jesus Christ.

You send us out, living God,
    to be ambassadors of the gospel.
Help us to proclaim the King's message
    with faithfulness and joy
and may it please you
    to bless our proclamation with spiritual fruit.

Response

L: Creator God, you have bestowed on us your Spirit.

R: **Help us to show his fruit of love, joy and peace.**

Prayer for Peace

Go into a world of need to give
Go into a world of hunger to share
Go into a world of despair to care
Go in love and may God go with you.

Day 48

In the beginning of time I find God
In the end of time I find God
Beyond the reach of time I find God
In the immensity of eternity I know God.

Psalm 65.5–8   **Prayer for the Day**   **Reading:** John 16.16–22

Meditation words: *You will grieve, but your grief will turn to joy.*

Lord Jesus,
    there are times when we are faced with sorrow,
        when we go through the long vigil
            with someone who suffers and dies;
        when we see the pain and hunger
            of an oppressed people.
Your disciples experienced sorrow
        when you were taken from them.
But the sorrow of the evening went
        in the joy of the resurrection morning.
Help us to believe
        that one day all wrongs will be righted,
        all pain and suffering will be ended,
        that you will be one with your people
        in an abundant feast of joy.

Spirit of God,
    help us to clothe ourselves
        with compassion, kindness and patience,
        to be forgiving as we are forgiven,
        to show the love
        which binds everything together in perfect harmony
        so that we may be people of peace
            serving the Prince of Peace.

Send us out in faith, dear Jesus,
        knowing that if we proclaim your word
            we shall by your grace see fruit
        as surely as the sower of the seed
            knows that one day there will be reaping.

Response

L: Father, there are times when all seems dark in the evening of
    suffering;

R: Yet we can be confident in the joy of a new dawn.

Prayer for Peace

May the rain from heaven fall upon your fields
May the sun from heaven warm your growing crops
May the wind from heaven sweep through your life
And may the Lord of heaven bless you, your family and friends.

Day 49

You are the ground of my being, the heart of my love
You are the hope of my planning, the centre of my life
You are the dove of my peace, the core of my confidence
You are my love, my life, my Saviour and my God.

Psalm 65.9–13   Prayer for the Day   Reading: John 16.23–28

Meditation words: *Ask and you will receive, and your joy will be complete.*

Our faith is so small, Lord Jesus,
    and our expectations so limited.
We can come to the Father through you
    and ask anything and he will give it to us.
Our faith is small as a grain of mustard seed
    but we do believe, Lord Jesus;
so guide us to ask in your name
    that we may experience your miracle of grace
    and that our joy may know no bounds.

Lord our God,
    around us is the darkness of disbelief and the power of evil.
Guard us from responding to evil with evil
    and allowing temptation to overcome us.
Help us in the church to be at peace among ourselves
    and to seek peace in the world.
May we greet each other with the kiss of peace
    and offer our neighbours the sign of peace.
God of peace,
    make us pure and good
      and may we so work for the kingdom
      that we may welcome our Lord Jesus
        when he returns.

Send us out in hope, risen Redeemer,
knowing that when we are loyal witnesses
our hope is a vision for the future,
assurance of things not yet experienced
and a foretaste of the joy of heaven.

Response

L: Help us, dear Lord, to have the faith to ask

R: And we shall see the miracle of grace.

Prayer for Peace

May your path go through the forest of joy
May your way lead through the fields of kindness
May your road ascend the mountains of praise
May your pilgrimage pass by the rivers of peace.

Day 50

To be with you, precious Redeemer, is like the taste of sweetest
*   honey*
To taste you is like the choicest of fine wine
To drink of you refreshment from cool clear water
A taste beyond description, truly divine.

Psalm 66.1–6   **Prayer for the Day**   **Reading:** John 16.29–33

Meditation words: *I have told you these things, so that in me you*
may have peace. In this world you will have trouble. But take
heart! I have overcome the world.

Crucified Jesus,
        there are in our lives times of testing;
    we wonder why we cannot go forward
            or why we suffer or face loss.
    But you remind us that you have the victory.
    Your resurrection heralds our celebration.
    Whatever difficulty or suffering we experience,
            in you we find peace,
            that inner peace
            which no tribulation in the world can take away.
    You are one with the Father and the Spirit
            and by your grace we are with you.

God of living water,
        we pray for all those who suffer because of the lack of water;
            for farmers who see crops wither
                    for lack of irrigation;
            for mothers who see children die
                    because of water-borne diseases;
            for old people dying in pain
                    because of thirst and unclean water.

Inspire your people to work together
     to provide drinking water wherever it is needed.
So may we share the water of life.

Send us out in love, Friend and Brother,
     for love is at the heart of creation,
     love is the message we proclaim,
     love is the fulfilment of the law,
          love is your story in redemption.
Love communicates where languages divide
     and love is the language of heaven itself.

Response

L: Father, when we come to a time of testing

R: Give us strength to stand firm and keep faith.

Prayer for Peace

> *May the Father surround you with a circle of care*
> *May the Son surround you with a circle of love*
> *May the Spirit surround you with a circle of power*
> *May the blessed Trinity encircle you each day.*

The Teaching of Jesus

Day 51

Listen to the rush of the wind across the desert
Listen to the river as it courses over rocks
Listen to the ceaseless surge of the sea along the shore
Listen to the voice of God in the inner depth of your being.

Psalm 67   **Prayer for the Day**   **Reading:** Luke 4.14–30

Meditation words: *Today this scripture is fulfilled in your hearing.*

Loving Jesus,
    you speak with such authority
    and startle us by your challenge.
Deliver us from prejudice and narrowness;
    deliver us from hatred and enmity.
Inspire us to accept the people of all nations
    as brothers and sisters in your name.
May we strive together to make our world
    a place of freedom, of health, of love.
May your peace in our hearts and lives
    become good news for the poor
    and an announcement of hope.

Healer Jesus,
    we pray for all those who suffer
    because of muscular dystrophy and multiple sclerosis.
Many have suffered through many years
    and endure great pain and difficulty.
Guide all those who conduct research,
    seeking a cure for such terrible diseases.
Give strength and help to the relatives
    who care for the sufferers with such love and loyalty.

Stretch out your hand to heal
    so that those who seem without hope
     may be given hope.
May the day soon come
    when a cure is found for these diseases
      and joy be brought into the lives of many families.

I give you this minute, Lord, a minute of time.
I offer this minute gift, Lord, an offering of time.
Yet in this minute is eternity
    for in this present moment I offer you myself
      in response to your eternal gift of grace.

Response

L: When we feel lost in the maze of modern life

R: **Lord, guide us into your way of eternal truth.**

Prayer for Peace

May the sun shed its radiance upon you
May the breezes blow freshly around you
May showers of abundant rain fall upon you
May the Holy Trinity bless you day by day.

Day 52

Each petal has a beauty that defies description
Each leaf is fashioned with delicate care
Each stem and stalk carries life through its core
Each flower has the signature of God.

Psalm 68.4–6   **Prayer for the Day**   **Reading:** Luke 6.20–36

Meditation words: *Rejoice in that day and leap for joy.*

Divine Teacher,
>you challenge us so much by your words.
>We are rich compared to many in the world
>>yet we often lack generosity to the poor;
>we have plenty of food compared to the hungry
>>yet we often fail to share our blessings with others;
>we live in a world of much enmity and division
>>yet we fail in offering our love to overcome enmity.
>Forgive us and help us to be true to your teaching,
>>to love as you love,
>>to give expecting nothing in return,
>>to help in building a new world of compassion and
>>>mutual care.

Holy Jesus,
>you delighted in the company of children.
>We pray for children, especially those in need.
>Guide and bless those who care for them,
>>parents, child minders, the staff in homes;
>may they count it a privilege and joy
>>to care for the little ones you have committed to them.
>Where there has been deep trauma and suffering
>>we pray that there may be a special deep love
>>which will help in the process of healing.

May all those who care for children
    teach them something about you
    in the love they express.

Peace is your promise, Lord;
    fruit of the Spirit,
    harvest of righteousness,
    found in your presence,
    enfolding us, upbuilding us, encircling us.
Peace is your gift, Lord.

Response

L: Divine Creator, when we go through a deep winter of despair

R: Renew in us the springtime of life, health and hope.

Prayer for Peace

*May you be blessed with courage like Abraham
    as you take your journey of faith
May you be blessed with vision like Jacob
    when he saw the ladder from earth to heaven
May you be blessed with wisdom like Joseph
    who became a blessing for his people
May you be blessed by God, creator of heaven and earth.*

Day 53

The night sky darkens, reminder of primaeval chaos
The stars shine bright, symbols of prophetic voices
The moon illumines all, as the Christ banishes darkness
So may we find fullness of light in God.

Psalm 68.7–10   **Prayer for the Day**   **Reading:** Luke 7.18–28

Meditation words: *Go back and report to John what you have seen and heard.*

Healer Jesus,
    we give you thanks for your ministry on earth
        when you healed the sick and gave sight to the blind.
    We give you thanks that you commission us
        to proclaim the good news and to heal the sick.
    Go with us on our journeys of witness;
        enable us in our ministry of healing and helping;
        grant us the joy of witnessing the lame walking,
            the blind seeing and the deaf hearing.
    May we share the joy of the poor and the hungry
        who hear your gospel and walk with you.
    May we find our peace in announcing that good news.

Lord God,
    there is something especially beautiful
        about a face that is lined with age.
    Every wrinkle, every furrow, seems to speak of their story
        and is a reminder of their rich and varied experiences.
    There is so much of suffering and joy
        in a life that spans generations.
    Be with those who have reached the evening of life
        that they may have happiness in remembering
        and no fear in looking to the future.

As they have given so much to others
so may they receive loving care from the new generation
and experience in your presence
deep and lasting peace.

Servant Jesus,
you taught us so wonderfully
in your actions as well as your words.
So you took the towel and the basin of water
and washed the dusty feet of your disciples.
May we consider no task too humble, no job too mean,
no office too lowly to undertake for your kingdom.
So may we be the servant people
ready at all times to follow and obey
our Servant King.

Response

L: Lord of the oceans, when we face a time of stormy waters

R: **Guide us by your grace into the calm waters of new seas.**

Prayer for Peace

Let the fire of enthusiasm be in your heart
Let the wisdom of scripture be in your mind
Let the joy of the Spirit be in your life
Let the peace of the Son surround you always
Let the love of the Father enfold you to eternity.

Day 54

Son of God, you are my light
Holy Jesus, you are my Saviour
Loving Christ, you are my Lord
Walk with me on the pilgrim way.

Psalm 68.15–18   **Prayer for the Day**   **Reading: Luke 8.4–15**
Meditation words: *He who has ears to hear, let him hear.*

Dear Lord,
    you call us to follow you and we have responded with joy.
    Forgive us for the times when we have failed you,
        when we have yielded to temptation,
        when we have lacked depth in faith,
        when we have given way to anxiety.
    Keep us faithful to you in all that lies ahead
        that we may bear fruit for your kingdom.

Divine Creator,
    we look with wonder at the loveliness of a bird in flight
        and we have longed for something of the same freedom.
    We thank you that by the skill of many people
        we are able to mount up with wings as eagles,
        that we can fly speedily from one nation to another.
    Bless the pilots, air hostesses and other crew members
        who care for those who travel by aeroplanes.
    Let us count it a privilege
        that we can enjoy the sensation of being above the
                clouds,
        can look down on mountain tops far below
        and can view mighty rivers as veins in the landscape.
    For such indescribable beauty may your name be praised.

Holy Jesus,
>   what a wonderful experience you gave to your disciples
>   when you shared together in the passover feast.
>   You broke the bread and passed it to your friends;
>   you poured the wine and shared it with your disciples.
>   In that mystic moment they were made one with you
>   and beyond the bounds of time
>   your body and your blood
>   united them and you
>   with your followers in every generation.
>   So may we enter into that mystery;
>   each time we receive the bread and wine at communion
>   may we know ourselves one with you and all your people.

Response

L: Lord, there are times when I am in the valley of doubt, and
occasions when I am on the mountain-top of faith;

**R: Help me to know in joy and sorrow, in health or sickness, in
the valleys and on the mountains, that you are with me.**

Prayer for Peace

*May the song of the nightingale be a blessing to you
May the flight of the dove be a blessing to you
May the song of the lark be a blessing to you
May the great Creator of all living beings bless you now and
always.*

Day 55

The candle burns brightly, the candle of peace
The star shines with radiance, the star of peace
The sun blazes with splendour, the sun of peace
But outshining all in glory, the Prince of Peace,
        Jesus our Lord.

Psalm 68.19–20   **Prayer for the Day**

Reading: Luke 9.23–27 & 57–62

Meditation words: *Whoever loses his life for me will save it.*

Saviour Jesus,
        you held nothing back
                but gave your life as a ransom for your people;
        such was the depth and wonder of your love.
        Help us to respond to you in faith
                even if it be as a grain of mustard seed.
        Not all the wealth of the Americas
                nor any position of power in the nations of the world
                can compare with the joy of belonging to your
                                                kingdom.
        Help us to put aside temptations and anxieties
                and so to serve you faithfully in this life
                that we might be welcomed by you
                        in the glory of your heavenly kingdom.

Holy Father,
        we thank you for our planet earth
                and for all the good things which it produces.
        We pray for all those who work on the land,
                for farmers and farm employees,
                for soil researchers and makers of agricultural
                                                machinery.

May they find fufilment in producing food
  that gives sustenance and joy to so many people.
May we who are fortunate in having so much food
  be ready to share it with those facing famine and
                                               hunger.
May all the people join in the harvest songs
  that give you praise and thanks for all your gifts.

Working for the good of all, Creator;
  make us a new creation.
Walking for the common welfare, Pilgrim;
  go with us on our way.
Weakened for the world's salvation, Redeemer;
  keep us mindful of your cross.
Whispering to our inner self, Lover;
  enfold us in communion with you.

Response

L: Holy Redeemer, there are times when we are lost in doubt and
   hopelessness;

R: **But you give us renewed hope as you lead us in the way of
   faith.**

Prayer for Peace

May the scent of the rose be a blessing to you
May the sound of the bees be a blessing to you
May the sight of the swallows be a blessing to you
May the voice of God, Father, Son and Spirit, be a blessing to you.

Day 56

Be still and know that God is with you
Be still and know that his life is all around
Be still and know that the planet shows God's splendour
Be still and know that all is and will be well.

Psalm 68.32–35   **Prayer for the Day**   **Reading:** Luke 9.1–6
                                      & 10.1–9

Meditation words: *Heal the sick who are there and tell them,*
'The kingdom of God is near you.'

Holy Redeemer,
    you have called us to proclaim your name in word and
                                             action;
        help us to be faithful to our calling.
Inspire us in the announcement of your love;
empower us in healing the sick and helping the needy;
may we spare no effort in preaching the kingdom of God;
may we have the assurance that you are with us
        and that you will continue as our companion
                in all our pilgrimage.

Lord God,
    we have seen the blight
        that can be caused in towns and cities by bad planning;
we recall the suffering of generations in the slums;
we see how the same hardship is found in our own time.
May we be blessed with planners who have vision,
        who plan villages, towns and cities
        that encourage community care and mutual support.
May we learn the lessons of the past
        as we plan for a future bright with promise
            not for a chosen few but for all people.

May that vision extend beyond our own nation
    and encompass the global village
    in which we all live and are connected to each other.

Loving Jesus,
    we make our protest with Peter; we will never betray you.
    We will lay down our lives for you.
    But when the time of testing comes,
        in weakness, cowardice and shame,
        we betray you; we deny your name.
    Forgive us, Lord.
    Help us to be courageous.
    Give us a new beginning
        and help us, like Peter, to become a rock
        in faith and in love.

Response

L: Lord of heaven and earth, the saints and angels praise your
    name;

R: God of sea and sky, all your creatures and all your people join
    in the song of praise.

Prayer for Peace

May the God who divided day from night bless you
May the God who said 'Let there be light' bless you
May the God who divided land from water bless you
May the Creator of the heavens and earth bless you now and
    always.

Day 57

Lord, go with us on life's journey
You have been with us at the beginning of the road
Guide us at each parting of the ways
Be with us at the journey's end.

Psalm 69.13–17   **Prayer for the Day**   **Reading:** Luke 10.25–37

Meditation words: *Jesus told him, 'Go and do likewise.'*

Dearest Friend,
    you have taught us how to care for one another
        because you love all your people, however undeserving
                                        we are.
    Help us to serve those in need, whether near or far;
        may we count it a privilege to give to those who are
                                        poor;
        may we count it an honour to give food to the hungry;
        may the door of our home be open to the deprived;
        may no effort or cost be too great
        in responding to any crisis amongst the people of our
                                        district.
    May our love be an expression of your love
        reaching out into the heart of the community.

Living God,
    we give you thanks that you speak to us
        through your word expressed in holy scriptures.
    Guide with your wisdom all translators and interpreters
        of those precious scriptures.
    Give courage and continued faith to those who distribute
                                        them,
        even when it is risky and dangerous to do so.

Bless the work of the Bible Society and all who share in this
noble task
of passing on to others the good news they have
received.

Risen Lord, the sign of your presence was the gift of peace.
When your disciples met you
they received the greeting of peace
and were filled with wonder.
Risen Lord, the sign of your presence is the gift of peace.
When we meet you in worship or on the mountain top
your words of greeting fill our hearts with peace
and we joyfully proclaim your name to our
generation.
Risen Lord, the sign of your presence will be peace
when you come again in glory to judge all people
and to receive your chosen into the joy of your
eternal kingdom.

Response

L: Loving Shepherd, as you guide your sheep over mountain
paths to the safety of the fold

R: **So you bring us from the places of danger to the safe haven of
your presence.**

Prayer for Peace

May God, maker of the great creatures, walk with you
May God, maker of the small creatures, go with you
May God, maker of the sea creatures, speak with you
May God, maker of the birds of the air, hear your prayers
May the God of all living creatures bless you now and always.

Day 58

The lark's call above the distant hill
The eagle soaring beyond the far peak
The hawk hovering high over the scrubland
The dove brooding deep in the wood
All speak the praise of our Creator.

Psalm 69.30–35a **Prayer for the Day** **Reading:** Luke 11.1–10

Meditation words: *Seek and you will find.*

Father in heaven,
    we glorify your name and thank you for all your love;
        may we see the signs of your kingdom all around us.
    Forgive us for our times of weakness;
    strengthen us in times of temptation;
    help us to forgive those who have wronged us.
    Inspire us to share our bread with the hungry,
        to share our homes with the homeless,
        to share our resources with the poor.
    Go with us on our journey of discovery
        and help us to know that you are with us always
            to the end of the age.
    We pray in the name of Jesus Christ our Lord.

Divine Musician,
    we give thanks for all who praise you
        in music and in songs, with instruments and voices.
    Bless all those in choirs and orchestras
        that by their skill they may please others
        and add to the sum of the world's loveliness.
    As the choir of heavenly angels praises you
        so may your people on earth express in harmony
            our worship and adoration.

What some can express so beautifully in song
    may we all express in lives dedicated to you,
so that our compassion and mutual care
    may be a pleasing symphony to you.

Loving parent,
    we pray for parents today.
    Children are a precious gift
        and face many risks in our society.
    Give to parents wisdom to teach the truth,
        compassion to give care with sensitivity,
        firmness in discipline and gentleness in love.
    May they, by word and example, bring up their children
        in the joy of faith in Christ.

Response

L: God of the living water, when we pass through times of aridity
    and thirst

R: We can trust you to bring us to wells of the refreshing water of
    life.

Prayer for Peace

May the mystery of the Three surround you
    when you rest in the shade of the tree
    when you climb the mountain's crest
    when you swim in the ocean's depths
May the mystery of the Three surround you.

Day 59

I offer you my eyes, Lord; be in my looking
I offer you my ears, Lord; be in my hearing
I offer you my tongue, Lord; be in my speaking
I offer you my hands, Lord; be in my working.

Psalm 70.4–5   **Prayer for the Day**   **Reading:** Luke 12.13–24

Meditation words: *A man's life does not consist in the abund-ance of his possessions.*

Loving Jesus,
    you have taught us that life in the Spirit
        is careful of others
            and careless of our own comforts,
        is generous towards the needy
            and economical for ourselves,
        is abundant in offering to God
            and sparing in self-indulgence.
Inspire us to put our trust in you
    and to know that we shall not be disappointed.
Let us look around
    at the beauty of the daffodil and butterfly
    and be filled with joy
    that God who created their beauty
    will care no less for us in meeting our true needs.
As the Father has been so abundant in his giving to us
    so may we be open-handed in our giving to others.
Above all help us to seek your kingdom
    for in this way we shall find our happiness and
                      fulfilment.

Lord of all creation,
    we praise you for the beauty of forests and woods,
        for the loveliness of trees in spring and autumn.

We pray for all forestry workers
    that by their understanding and skill
    they may preserve the heritage we have received
        in the great forests of our generation
    and may plant new trees for future generations.
We pray for all with responsibility
    for the great rain forests of Brazil
        and for other areas of great natural resources.
Help us to take better care of the planet you have given us.
May the trees of the fields clap their hands
    and all your people go out with joy and peace.

The rhythm of life, sunrise and sunset, dawn and dark
Flow of the seas, tide in, tide out
Flow of our faith, eagerness, aridity
The rhythm of discipleship, denial and affirmation
Lord God, you are with us, in light and dark,
    the Spirit uniting us with you and your Son.

Response

L: We worship God on the hilltops, in gardens and beside lakes.

R: **We worship God in the shopping centres, in busy streets and market squares.**

Prayer for Peace

As the rain falls from heaven on the hills
As the streams flow down to join the river
As the rivers run down to join the sea
So may you find blessing in communion with God.

Day 60

At the centre of stillness, we find our God
At the heart of meditation, we meet our Creator
At the crux of all life's story, we encounter our Redeemer
At the fullness of time, we meet our Maker
At the centre of stillness we find our God.

Psalm 71.1–8   **Prayer for the Day**   **Reading:** Luke 14.7–14

Meditation words: *He who humbles himself will be exalted.*

Loving Redeemer,
    you were the Lord of the universe
        but you made yourself nothing
            for the sake of your people;
        you emptied yourself of glory to offer us eternal life.
    Help us to have the same mind as you had,
        to count others better than ourselves
        and to make ourselves available
            for the work of your kingdom.

Living Vine,
    you delighted in the quiet of a garden
        and we share with you that sense of peace in gardens.
    We ask for your inspiration and blessing
        for all those who plan gardens and work in them;
        for landscape gardeners, workers in orchards,
        those who grow flowers
            and all who help to surround us
                with the beauty of cultivated gardens.
    May we in thankfulness for all this loveliness
        seek to bring a like beauty into the lives of those
        who have little opportunity to see the beauty of nature
            or share in the joy of gardens.
    So may our lives show the splendour of the flowers.

Loving Shepherd,
    we give you thanks that you care for your people,
        being ready to sacrifice your life for our sakes.
    You are the good Shepherd;
        you know your sheep by name
            and care for all individually.
    When danger threatens you are there to protect;
        when sheep wander away and are lost
        you search until you find them
            and then return them to the fold.
    You care for your sheep whatever the cost
        and you draw us together
            so we are one flock, one shepherd.

Response

L: When the church is tested by the fires of persecution

R: The Holy Spirit enables the saints to endure to the end.

Prayer for Peace

As the candle burns bright in a dark cave
As the stars cast light on dark streets
As the sun by its dawning scatters the darkness
So may the light of God illumine your life.

Day 61

Weave, Lord, weave your holiness into our lives
Weave, Lord, weave your wisdom into our minds
Weave, Lord, weave your love into our hearts
Weave something of yourself into the warp and woof of our
    being.

Psalm 71.15–18   **Prayer for the Day**   **Reading:** Luke 14.15–24

Meditation words: *But they all alike began to make excuses.*

Lord Jesus,
    you have called us to follow you.
    Deliver us from making excuses;
        help us to overcome the temptation
           to take another way.
    May we find our joy in responding to your call
        and our peace in the presence of our heavenly Father.

Shepherd Jesus,
    you care for your flock.
    You care also for all in the animal world,
        squirrels, beavers, badgers and foxes,
        dogs, cats, hamsters and donkeys.
    As your Father created all the animal species
        and took delight in naming them,
           so you show your care for animals, wild and tame.
    We confess that we have not always expressed that care;
        animals have been cruelly treated;
        whole species have been endangered by human hunting;
        elephants have been slaughtered for their tusks;
        calves have been killed to provide veal;
        the minx, the leopard and the fox
           have been sacrificed to provide a coat of fur.
    Forgive us for the faults of the past.

Bless all those societies that tend wounded animals
   and provide sanctuary for those that have suffered.
Help us to take better care of all the creatures
   you have committed to us in stewardship.

All over the world your people are praising you, God of the
                                                    universe
      with the drums of Africa, worshipping God;
      with the violins of Europe, praising God;
      in the varied voices of the Americas, worshipping God;
      with the harmony of Asia, praising God;
May all the world glorify you, the God of creation.

Response

L: Divine Potter, you take such broken pots as we are to use for
   your divine purpose.

R: **Break us and remake us for the work of your kingdom, mould
   us and reshape us for the glory of your name.**

Prayer for Peace

May the Father bless you with wisdom in your words
May the Son bless you with compassion in your actions
May the Spirit bless you with joy in your service
May God, Father, Son and Spirit, bless you now and always.

In our rising each new day, praise to God
In the doing of our daily work, praise to God
In the eating of our daily meals, praise to God
In our entering into the rest of night, praise to God.

Psalm 71.19–23　　**Prayer for the Day**　　**Reading:** Luke 15.1–10

Meditation words: *There is rejoicing in the presence of the angels of God over one sinner who repents.*

Loving Shepherd,
　　we give you thanks for your loving care
　　　　in searching for your lost sheep.
　　No one is forgotten by you, none written off as worthless.
　　When we go astray you pursue us;
　　　　when we are lost you search until we are found.
　　Help us to care about others as you care for us;
　　　　inspire us to share the good news of your love.
　　Whenever anyone turns from the failings of the past
　　　　and trusts you for all that lies ahead
　　then we join our song with the songs of the angels
　　　　and we share in the joy of heaven.

God of travellers,
　　we pray for all those who help us to travel safely,
　　　　especially for taxi drivers who take people to their
　　　　　　　　　　　　　　　　　　　　　　　　destinations
　　　　by day, by night, in joyful excursions, in times of
　　　　　　　　　　　　　　　　　　　　　　　　　crisis.
　　Protect them in their journeys.

May they never abuse the trust placed in them;
may their knowledge and skill be used for the common good;
may they find satisfaction not only in wages and tips,
> but much more in work well done in service to others
> and for the honour of your name.

Risen Jesus,
> you are the resurrection and the life;
>> whoever believes in you does not die
>>> but enters into the life that is eternal.
> This is the good news we share with all people —
>> that death does not have dominion over us;
>>> death is not an end but a door to new life.
> You have opened for us the gates of life
>> so we can look forward to perpetual joy.
> Inspire us to proclaim that good news
>> to all who are ready to hear
>>> that they may believe and have eternal life.

Response

L: King of love, when we experience conflict, hostility and violence

R: Keep us faithful and lead us to the place of peace.

Prayer for Peace

May the Father inspire you with the gift of love
May the Son enliven you with the gift of joy
May the Spirit enfold you with the gift of peace
May God, Father, Son and Spirit, abide with you always.

Day 63

Wind the thread of hope, Lord, and bind the thread of joy
Wind the thread of kindness, Lord, and bind the thread of love
Wind the thread of patience, Lord, and bind the thread of peace
When we are bound to you, Lord, we find the thread of life.

Psalm 72.1–6   **Prayer for the Day**   **Reading:** Luke 15.11–32

Meditation words: *This brother of yours was dead and is alive again; he was lost and is found.*

Lord of the Dance,
　　we give you thanks that in your name we can celebrate.
　　We celebrate the beauty of creation;
　　　　we celebrate the depth and breadth of your love;
　　　　we celebrate that you have drawn so many people to
　　　　　　　　　　　　　　　　　　　　　　　　yourself;
　　　　we celebrate that so many have found new life in you;
　　　　we celebrate the gift of your Holy Spirit.
　　We join with the saints of every age,
　　　　with angels and archangels,
　　　　to celebrate our fellowship in your kingdom.

Loving Jesus,
　　we ask your blessing on all social workers,
　　　　especially those concerned with the welfare of families.
　　There is so much hurt where there has been violence;
　　　　there is so much trauma where there is breakdown;
　　　　there is so much suffering in bereavement.
　　Give patience, understanding and skill
　　　　to all those working alongside families,
　　　　seeking to bring about reconciliation,
　　　　helping to build bridges of understanding,
　　　　giving comfort where it is needed
　　　　　　and encouragement where there has been despair.

May they know that what they do for those in such need
they do for you.

Deep underground, in great caverns,
we see your beauty, Lord God.
Deep under the seas, in hidden crevices,
we see your glory, divine Creator.
Deep in space, on far planets,
people sense your presence, God of eternity.
Deep in our inner being,
we hear your voice, God of the mystic moment.

Response

L: Divine Physician, when your people go through times of
suffering, pain and sickness

**R: May your healing hands touch them, bless them and lift their
spirits.**

Prayer for Peace

May the Father grant you the gift of patience
May the Son grant you the gift of kindness
May the Spirit grant you the gift of goodness
May God, Father, Son and Spirit, bless you day by day.

Day 64

Take away the tensions, Lord, and ease away the cares
Help us to relax, Lord, and drive away our fears
Come close to us; keep evil out and banish darkness
Grant us your forgiveness, your peace and righteousness.

Psalm 72.1, 15–19 **Prayer for the Day** **Reading:** Luke 16.19–30

Meditation words: *Now he is comforted here and you are in agony.*

Jesus, light of the world,
    we give you thanks that you came into our world,
        died and rose again to offer us eternal life.
    Forgive us that we have sometimes been indifferent
        to the claims of your kingdom.
    Grant us inspiration to live as children of light,
        proclaiming the good news to those around us
            and sharing in the joy when some respond.
    May your light scatter the darkness around us
        and illumine the path of all who seek you.

Lord God,
    we hold before you a world of need,
        in which many face hunger, many have lost homes,
        many are refugees and many experience violence.
    We ask your guidance and blessing
          for all who work and raise funds
        that the hungry may be fed, the homeless housed,
        refugees given a welcome and victims of war helped.
    We pray for Christian Aid, Cafod and Tear Fund
        and many other organizations
            active in world development projects.
    Give them vision and faith in their work of compassion.

May they know that in giving a cup of water to any,
in sinking a well for a village,
in funding an agricultural project for a region,
they are doing this for you and bring joy to heaven.

Holy Spirit,
give us the spiritual fruit of peace;
the peace that cares for the wellbeing of all people;
the peace that rebukes injustice and violence;
the peace that seeks freedom for all;
the peace that heals the hurts of the past;
the peace that enables for today
and releases the potential for tomorrow;
the peace that is new life in Christ.

Response

L: Lord of the changing seasons, by your divine grace there is
morning and evening, ebb and flow;

R: Grant us your blessing in our coming and going, in our youth
and age, in our morning and our evening of life.

Prayer for Peace

May the Father bless you with the gift of faithfulness
May the Son inspire in you the quality of gentleness
May the Spirit enable you to exercise self-control
May God, Father, Son and Spirit, bless you this day and always.

Day 65

Come into a place apart and listen to God
Come into the sanctuary and look for God
Come into the holy of holies and wait on God
Be still and in the silence know that God is here.

Psalm 74.12–17   **Prayer for the Day**   **Reading:** Luke 18.1–8

Meditation words: *When the Son of Man comes, will he find faith on earth?*

Holy Father,
    we wait on you with a sense of longing.
    Draw us to yourself and help us to know
        the depth and wonder of your love.
    We come before you with assurance
        because we know that Jesus intercedes for us.
    We hold before you a world of need and hunger;
    we hold before you relatives and friends who are ill;
    we hold before you people on a spiritual search.
    Reach to them through your Spirit
        that they may know your help, your healing, your
                         support.
    Hear the prayer we offer you in Jesus' name.

Divine Redeemer,
    we live in a world of so much violence
        and in so many places people are deprived of human
                         rights.
    We pray for all those who face torture or imprisonment
        because they speak and act for what is just and true.

We give thanks for the work of many organizations
    which are active in the field of human rights,
        for Amnesty International, the Defence and Aid Fund
            and others with a like concern.
May they bring light in dark places;
    may they bring hope where there has been despair.
By their activities may those who felt themselves forgotten
    know that there are those who care.
May your presence be their constant inspiration.

Creator Spirit,
    you are within us and around us;
        by your power the universe has being;
        in your love the world is blessed;
        to you we come for guidance with trust.
    Help us in the daily struggle of life
        and in the great spiritual conflict with darkness
    to live day by day the life of discipleship
        and to range ourselves alongside your power and light.

Response

L: Holy God, as you gave the sign of the burning bush to Moses

R: **So may we see signs of your holy presence all around us.**

Prayer for Peace

May God the great Spirit accompany your journeying
May God the Mother of all being watch over your progress
May God the spark of all life ignite your enthusiasm
May the triune God, the great mystery, give you a benediction.

Day 66

Turn away sin, Lord, and turn away sorrow
Turn away hate, Lord, and turn away quarrels
Bind us together in harmony and joy
Seal us with your Spirit in a life of light and peace.

Psalm 75.1–3   **Prayer for the Day**   **Reading:** Luke 18.9–17

Meditation words: *Everyone who exalts himself will be humbled, and he who humbles himself will be exalted.*

Lord Jesus,
    forgive us for our boasting and self-satisfaction;
    forgive us for our pride, envy and greed;
    forgive us for the secret sins we hide from others;
    forgive us for our denial of you.
    Help us to be child-like in our trust,
        to follow you knowing that you will never fail us,
        to wait for you knowing that you will guide us,
        to pray to you knowing that you will answer us.
    Challenge us by your teaching,
        inspire us in discipleship by your ministry,
        bring us at the last to the joy of your heavenly kingdom
        where with all the saints and angels
        we may praise and worship our Father and Friend.

Teacher Jesus,
    you have called people into the work of ministry
        and they need preparation for their precious task.
    We pray for all who teach in our theological colleges.
    May they be people of faith and vision,
        firmly grounded in the scriptures,
        inspired by your teaching and ministry,
        imbued with wisdom through your Holy Spirit.

May they find fulfilment and happiness
>in preparing men and women to preach the gospel,
>>to celebrate the sacraments,
>>to serve the community and to care for your church
>>>for the glory of your Father.

Peace is found in the completing of tasks
>and in the responding to your will, Lord God.
Help us to be faithful in discipleship,
>to be content in all the circumstances
>into which you lead us.
May we by the peace of our inner being
>help to bring peace to others.

Response

L: Lord God, you go before us as a pillar of cloud by day;

R: You guide us by the pillar of fire by night.

Prayer for Peace

The God of yesterday has done great things for you
The God of today shows great signs for you
The God of tomorrow will perform great wonders for you
The God of eternity, Father, Son and Spirit, bless you now and
>*always.*

Day 67

Silently I sit in the presence of God
Quietly I wait for the word of the Lord
Peacefully I receive the gift of the Spirit
Joyfully I rest in the blessed Trinity.

Psalm 77.1–6a   **Prayer for the Day**   **Reading:** Luke 19.11–27

Meditation words: *Because you have been trustworthy in a very small matter, take charge of ten cities.*

Righteous Lord,
    we give you thanks for all the gifts you have bestowed on us
        and the commission you give us.
Help us to be faithful servants,
    ready for the work of your kingdom,
    open to the leading of your Holy Spirit
    and loyal in our service and witness.
You have given to us without counting the cost.
May we respond to you with conscientious care
    so that we may prove good stewards
        of all that you have committed to us.

Living God,
    we give you thanks that you inspire your church
        to serve and witness in the power of your Spirit.
We pray for all those who are given tasks
    in the leadership, care and service of your people.
We pray for bishops, moderators and chairmen
    and other pastoral leaders in your church.
May they be people of humility, vision and faith
    seeking to equip the saints for work in your kingdom.

May they look to Jesus, the great Shepherd of the sheep,
   and find in him their inspiration
      for their service in pastoral care,
   for the glory of your name.

God of the pilgrim way,
   you have given the word of life.
   The news we bring is not of our making,
      the message we proclaim is not ours to change;
   we pass on that which we have received.
   Enable us by your Spirit
      to proclaim the love you have shown in your Son
   that people may hear and believe.

Response

L: Lord, we live our lives here on earth

R: But you set before us a ladder up to heaven.

Prayer for Peace

May you find deep stillness in your ocean journey
May you find deep quiet on the high mountain
May you find the inward silence of mystic contemplation
May the peace of the Blessed Trinity be yours to your life's
   fulfilment.

Day 68

Peace, in the doing of your will
Joy, in the building of your kingdom
Love, in the fellowship of your people
Fulfilment, in responding to your call.

Psalm 77.11–14   **Prayer for the Day**   **Reading:** Luke 20.9–18

Meditation words: *What then will the owner of the vineyard do to them?*

Holy God,
    you have put us in a pleasant vineyard
        and you call on us to show fruit for your kingdom.
    Help us to show such fruit in love, joy and peace
        as we seek to be your faithful stewards
            and servants of all for your sake.
    We have failed so often in the past
        in joining the company of those who reject you.
    Help us to turn to you and to find life;
    open to us the gates of righteousness
        that we may enter through them and give thanks to you.
    This is the day that you have made;
        help us to be full of joy and glad in it
        as we accept our salvation through Jesus Christ our Lord.

Dear Jesus,
    we know that our busy streets can be places of danger,
        especially for children and the elderly.
    We ask for your blessing on all traffic wardens
        as they seek to bring children and others
            safely across the road to school or home.

We ask your blessing on policemen and others
   who are responsible for crowd control,
      for policing motorways and other roads
         and for keeping a watch on homes and shops.
May they find satisfaction in their care for the community;
may they carry out their tasks with honesty and integrity;
may they prove worthy of the trust placed in them.
We pray in your precious name.

Holy Spirit,
   what a delight it is when someone comes to belief in Jesus
      through the word you have committed to us.
It is like the oasis in the desert,
      like the bright star in a dark sky,
      like the sensitive act of love
         in the callous cruelty of a concentration camp.
Draw your people to yourself through Jesus our Lord.

Response

L: Lord, with the stones of faith and hope and love

R: May we overcome the giants of despair and greed and hate.

Prayer for Peace

May the God of the changing seasons bless your years
May the God of all living creatures bless your journeys
May the God of sun, moon and stars bless your meditation
May God, Father, Son and Holy Spirit, bless you in discipleship.

Day 69

> *Lord, you are the journey's start*
> *You are the journey's road*
> *You are the journey's end*
> *Our beginning and our completing.*

Psalm 77.16–19   **Prayer for the Day**

Reading: Luke 21.10–19 & 25–28

Meditation words: *This will result in your being witnesses to them.*

Lord Jesus Christ,
    we give you thanks for your promise
        that you will come again gloriously
            to sum up world history
            and to call your people to the Feast.
    Help us to read the signs of the times.
    Inspire us that we may at all times have our lamps burning;
    Guard us from the snares, temptations and distractions
        of this world and of evil spiritual powers.
    Fill us with your Holy Spirit
        that we may walk as children of the light
        and be ready to welcome you at the time of your
                              arriving.
    Come, Lord Jesus; come quickly.

God of mercy,
    for many people life is constant crisis
        and the night brings no rest but more despair.
    Some have been hurt far in the past;
    some have passed through traumatic experience;
    some wrestle with mental pressures and stress.
    Be near to reassure them with your presence.

Bless the psychiatrists and nurses who care for them,
    listening with understanding,
    encouraging them to express themselves,
    allowing light to come where there was darkness,
    enabling the release of resentment and hate
    so that a process of healing and forgiveness may begin.
Lord Jesus,
    as you healed so long ago,
    so today may you bring healing of body, mind and
                                 spirit.

Father,
    grant us help through your Son
    to speak a word of comfort and of challenge;
    to witness to your power and your love;
    to share with people around us
        the joy that is ours in Christ.

Response

L: Holy God, when the way for us is hard and brings suffering

R: **Help us to remember your servant who gave his life as a ransom, suffering without complaint.**

Prayer for Peace

May the God of earthquake, wind and fire inspire you
May the God of the still small voice speak to you
May the God of mystic communion be one with you
May God, Father, Son and Spirit, be with you to your journey's
    end.

Day 70

Lord, where shall I go if I turn from you?
To whom shall I turn if I reject you?
On whom whall I rely if I deny you?
You have the word of eternal life;
Keep me faithful in your service.

Psalm 78.2–4   **Prayer for the Day**   **Reading:** Luke 22.14–23

Meditation words: *This is my body given for you . . . This cup is the new covenant in my blood, which is poured out for you.*

Loving Redeemer,
> we give you thanks that you took the road to Calvary
>> giving your life that you might offer us eternal life.
> We give you thanks for your presence with us
>> and for the way you meet with us in holy communion
>>> in the meal of fellowship.
>> when we recall your body broken and your blood shed.
> We pray that you will come to us when we celebrate the
>>>> sacrament
>> that we may spiritually feed upon you,
>> abiding in you as you abide in us.
> So may we be strengthened for our work in your kingdom
>> and have a foretaste of that heavenly banquet
>>> which we shall share with you and all God's people
>>> in the joy of our home in heaven.

Father,
> children are a precious gift in our community
>> and a treasured presence in the life of the church.
> We ask for your guidance and wisdom for all junior church
>>>> teachers.
> May they realize what an important and responsible task
>> has been committed to them in the care of the young.

May they give a good example by their life-style;
may they teach what is wholesome and true;
may they study your word and delight in sharing it;
may they have the joy of seeing many children come
    to fullness of faith and to discipleship.
So may your name be honoured
from generation to generation.

God of eternity,
    so often we think of death as struggle
        and the going over as a time of pain.
    Truly there can be pain in dying
        as in the agony of your Son on the cross.
    But he has also shown us
        that death is fulfilment, completion,
        and the passing over the threshold of death
            a transition to a more perfect life.
    This death is positive and good, a kind of healing too,
        a coming to the peace that passes understanding.

Response

L: Though friends may forsake us or relatives abandon us

**R: Lord, you are our faithful companion whose love never fails
    nor falters.**

Prayer for Peace

*As the sun in its shining brings glory
As the stars in the night scatter dark
As the moon gives us hope in its radiance
So may the light of God
    fill your heart and your mind and your life.*

Day 71

In the morning of hazy mists
In the noonday of blazing sun
In the evening of quiet shades
I worship the God of love.

Psalm 78.19b–20 & 23–25   **Prayer for the Day**

Reading: Luke 24.13–31

Meditation words: *Then their eyes were opened and they recognized him.*

Lord Jesus,
      when we break bread
            to offer to a hungry child in famine-striken Africa,
                  may we recognize you.
      When we take bread
            to offer to a tramp at our door,
                  may we recognize you.
      When we share bread
            by taking meals-on-wheels to an elderly pensioner,
                  may we recognize you.
      When we receive bread
            kneeling at the altar-rail,
                  may we recognize you.
      Meeting you, our risen Lord, may we receive your greeting
            'Peace be with you'
      and to our neighbours in sorrow and in joy
            may we too say 'Peace be with you.'

Loving Jesus,
      you knew what it was like
            to be deserted by all your friends and left alone.

We pray for all who experience loneliness;
> for those who live alone and are fearful;
> for those who have lost their life partner;
> for those who live in remote places;
> for those who are surrounded by people and yet feel
>> lonely.

May they come to find in the fellowship of your people
> a support that takes away loneliness
>> and replaces sadness with a new-found happiness.

May you be their constant companion,
> giving them inner peace and quiet assurance.

Father,
> so much conflict is within ourselves.
> Our jealousy, our pride, our passion,
>> our power-seeking and our greed
> all disturb the balance of life
>> and undermine the harmony of society.
> Forgive us, and lead us by your Spirit
>> that in our lives love may go hand in hand with peace,
>>> so filling our community with joy.

Response

L: God of the great seas, guide and protect us through the storms
> and the calm waters.

R: Lord of the oceans, pilot and direct us to secure ports and safe
> harbours.

Prayer for Peace

The maker of the silver fish, cascading shoal, be near you
The maker of the great fish, white whale, be around you
The maker of the gentle fish, playful dolphin, be close to you
May the Great Lord of sea creatures swim with you.

Day 72

We leave behind cares and anxieties
We step aside from worries and troubles
We come into the deep centre
and find fulfilment in meeting our God.

Psalm 80.8–15   **Prayer for the Day**   **Reading:** Luke 24.36–53

Meditation words: *You are witnesses of these things.*

Lord Jesus,
    you teach us so wonderfully all that we need to know
        concerning your Father and his kingdom
        and his great purpose of salvation for our world.
    You teach us also in your ministry of care,
        healing the sick, feeding the hungry
          and helping those in trouble and need.
    Inspire us to proclaim the good news to all nations.
    Enable us through your Holy Spirit to be witnesses
        to all that you have accomplished for your people.
    As we have received your blessing
        so may we announce a blessing for others
          as we go out with joy to share your peace.

Heavenly Father,
    we pray for your blessing for all those
        who are approaching the end of their life's journey,
        especially for any who go through a long vigil
        of suffering and pain.
    Be near to reassure them of your presence
        and may they know that Jesus will be beside them
          in their passing from this life to the next.

Bless with patience, wisdom and faith
　　all those who share this vigil
　　as doctors and nurses, as friends and relatives.
By their love and concern
　　may they surround their friend with light
　　and help them to overcome any fear
　　and to put their trust in you.
May we all know with full assurance
　　that you go with us through all our days
　　and you will bring us at the last
　　to the joy of your kingdom.

King Jesus,
　　by your inspiration help us to be servants of the kingdom.
　　May the world be filled with the splendour of your kingly
　　　　　　　　　　　　　　　　　　　　　　　　　　　rule.
　　For truly the kingdom of God is around us and within us;
　　　in your name, Jesus, the kingdom has come.

Response

L: God of the pilgrim way, speak to us on the holy mountain;

R: Prince of the path of peace, meet with us in the quiet garden.

Prayer for Peace

May the maker of light give light to your eyes
May the restorer of sight give sight to your eyes
May the guide of the inward seeing give depth to your eyes
May Father, Son and Spirit be in your seeing and your being.

Appendix

Prayers for the Day

SUNDAY: Prayer of St Francis

Lord, make me an instrument of your peace.
    Where there is hatred, let me sow love;
    where there is injury, pardon;
    where there is doubt, faith;
    where there is despair, hope;
    where there is darkness, light;
    where there is sadness, joy.
O divine Master,
    grant that I may not so much seek
        to be consoled as to console;
            to be understood as to understand;
        to be loved, as to love.
    For it is in giving that we receive,
        in pardoning that we are pardoned,
        and in dying that we are born to eternal life.

MONDAY: Prayer for the true love of peace

Almighty God,
    from whom all thoughts of truth and peace proceed;
    kindle, we pray, in the hearts of all people
        the true love of peace,
    and guide with your pure and peaceable wisdom
        those who take counsel for the nations of the world;
    that in tranquillity your kingdom may go forward,
        till the earth is filled with the knowledge of your love:
        through Jesus Christ our Lord.

based on Prayer Book 1928

TUESDAY: Prayer of St Patrick

May the strength of God pilot us;
may the power of God preserve us;
may the wisdom of God instruct us;
may the hand of God protect us;
may the way of God direct us;
may the shield of God defend us;
may the host of God guard us against the snares of the evil one
    and the temptations of the world.
May Christ be with us,
    Christ above us,
    Christ in us,
    Christ before us.
May your salvation, O Lord, be always ours
    this day and for evermore.

WEDNESDAY: The Light of Peace

We light this candle for peace, Lord.
    May its light scatter the darkness;
    may its flame be a symbol of hope;
    may its burning be a sign of faith
        joining with many other lights for peace.
We light this candle for peace.
    May our lives be an expression of peacemaking;
    may we seek to be lights in a dark world,
        pointing to you, Jesus, the Prince of Peace,
           and following you in the way of peace.
Let the candle burn, as a sign for peace,
        offered to you.

John Johansen-Berg

THURSDAY: Prayer of St Augustine

O God,
    from whom to be turned is to fall,
    to whom to be turned is to rise,
    and in whom to stand is to abide for ever;

151

Grant us
> in all our duties your help;
> in all our perplexities your guidance;
> in all our dangers your protection;
> and in all our sorrows your peace:
>> through Jesus Christ our Lord. Amen.

FRIDAY: **Prayer of St Richard**

Thanks be to you, my Lord Jesus Christ,
> for all the benefits which you have given me;
> for all the pains and insults which you have borne for me.
O most merciful Redeemer, Friend and Brother,
> may I know you more clearly,
>> love you more dearly,
>> and follow you more nearly
>>> day by day.

SATURDAY: **Prayer of St Benedict**

O Gracious and Holy Father,
> give us wisdom to perceive you,
>> diligence to seek you,
>> patience to wait for you,
>> eyes to behold you,
>> a heart to meditate upon you
>> and a life to proclaim you:
> through the power of the Spirit of Jesus Christ our Lord.
> Amen.

UNIVERSAL PRAYER FOR PEACE

Lord,
> lead me from death to life, from falsehood to truth;
> lead me from despair to hope, from fear to trust;
> lead me from hate to love, from war to peace.
> Let peace fill our heart, our world, our universe.
> Peace . . . . . Peace . . . . . Peace.